ALPHABETICAL
AFRICA

Also by Walter Abish

How German Is It (novel)
In the Future Perfect (fictions)
Minds Meet (short stories)

ALPHABETICAL AFRICA

by Walter Abish

A NEW DIRECTIONS BOOK

Manufactured in the United States of America
First published clothbound (ISBN: 0–8112–0532–0) and as
New Directions Paperbook 375 (ISBN: 0–8112–0533–9) in 1974.
Published simultaneously in Canada by Penguin Books Canada Limited.

New Directions Books are published for James Laughlin
by New Directions Publishing Corporation,
80 Eighth Avenue, New York 10011

SECOND PRINTING

For Cecile

ALPHABETICAL
AFRICA

AGES AGO, Alex, Allen and Alva arrived at Antibes, and Alva allowing all, allowing anyone, against Alex's admonition, against Allen's angry assertion: another African amusement . . . anyhow, as all argued, an awesome African army assembled and arduously advanced against an African anthill, assiduously annihilating ant after ant, and afterward, Alex astonishingly accuses Albert as also accepting Africa's antipodal ant annexation. Albert argumentatively answers at another apartment. Answers: ants are Ameisen. Ants are Ameisen?

Africa again: Antelopes, alligators, ants and attractive Alva, are arousing all angular Africans, also arousing author's analytically aggressive anticipations, again and again. Anyhow author apprehends Alva anatomically, affirmatively and also accurately.

Ages ago an archeologist, Albert, alias Arthur, ably attended an archaic African armchair affair at Antibes, attracting attention as an archeologist and atheist. Ahhh, atheism . . . anyhow, Albert advocated assisting African ants. Ants? All are astounded. Ants? Absurd.

Africa again: Albert arrives, alive and arguing about African art, about African angst and also, alas, attacking Ashanti architecture, as author again attempts an agonizing alphabetical appraisal . . . asked about affection, Albert answers, Ashanti affection also aesthetically abhorrent, antagonizing all. As alien airforce attacks Angola, Albert asks, are anthills anywhere about, agreeing as Alex asserts, all Angolans are absolute asses.

Are all archeologists arrogant Aristotelians, asks author, as Angolans abduct Alva. Adieu Alva. Arrivederci.

After air attack author assumes Alva's asexuality affected African army's ack-ack accuracy, an arguable assumption, anyhow, army advances, annihilating antelopes, alligators and ants. Admirable attrition admits Ashanti admiral as author all alone autographs Ashanti atlas, authenticating anthill actions. Actually, asks Alva, are all Ashanti alike.

Apprehending Africa: always, as an afternoon abates an ant advances, also antelopes, alligators, archeologists, African ankles, African amulets and amorous Angolan abductors. Abductors all agreed about abhorrent acts, about air attacks, about Alva and Alex and Allen all apart.

Africa again: Angolans applaud author, after author allegedly approached an American amateur aviator, and angrily argued against America's anachronistic assault. Afterward all applaud as author awarded avocado and appointed acting alphabet authority.

Alex and Allen alone, arrive in Abidjan and await African amusements.

BEFORE AFRICAN ADJOURNMENT, Alex, Allen and Alva arrive at Antibes, beginning a big bash, as August brings back a buoyancy, a belief, Ahhh, and believing all buy books about Angolan basins and about Burundi bathhouses, and a better, better, brotherhood, as both Alex and Allen bear Alva's anger . . . against brotherhood.

Africa as before: Bantu also admire beauty and abduct agreeable Alva, astonishing Alva, and by all accounts, always adapting and bending, beguiled by Bantu bedtime behavior, and by beautiful, bedazzling bedding, authentic batik.

Another Africa: books about black bureaucracy banned as Bantu begin another August by blowing Bach's baroque bugles, but after Bach's brother, Bach's blackguard brother Butoni, bemused by Bach, by Boccherini, Beethoven and Brahms, blunders a bit by baldly boasting about backing Beatles, Butoni's angry brother assaults and beats blabbering bullshit Butoni. Ahhh, August brings bitterness, brings busted branches, as Butoni, back badly bruised, badly beaten, badly bested and bleeding, borrows a big boat, and breaking anchor, as August blows a breeze, begins a broadening adventure. Baffled Bach asks abducted Alva's advice about brother. Banish Butoni, banish bastard Butoni.

3

Alex and Allen are both bribing a building attendant after building another apartment backstairs, but both also brood after burying a body, brood about Bantu's better beaches and accommodating Alva.

Alva arrives after ant atrocities, arrives bare breasted, a bit astonished as all assembled black bourgeoisie applaud Alva's bravery, and also auction a book about Afrikanische Ameisen. As before Butoni, baffled by books, by big business, by balling big brother, by Bantu beggars, again backs Beatles, but Beatles again are absent. By and by Butoni buys an Anglican bishop a beer. Both breathe African August air. Ahhh, both agree about bare-breasted Alva, bloody bad, and brood a bit, but briefly, barely, and also bitch about Bach, bloody bastard. Bishop amused at Butoni being Bach's brother, and Butoni allows bishop another amusement . . . blowing Bach's bugle, bishop blows beautiful bugle, breathing buoyant bulbul, before and after breakfast. Bye bye Beatles. But bastard Butoni brushes back bishop, annoyed, brushes back all benedictions. Bastard, bloody bastard.

Both Alex and Allen are back again at basement airport, and beset by African boredom, as American airforce bombs Ashanti beaches. After bombing, Butoni believes both are butchered, but both, bribing an aviator, borrow Bantu's airforce, arriving at Angola by afternoon. Begin big bash: aviators, bishop, author, British banker, architect, beverages, baklava, baked bananas.

Alex borrows beginners book about Bantu's behaviorism. Allen behaved badly.

C

CROSSING ANOTHER COUNTRY: Alex and Allen cajoling a bank clerk, come along, come along, convert captivating currency, clipping coupons and buy cheap cotton canopy containing cannabis. Coming by car colonialists avoid anthills, but are confronted by curious cannabis chewing custom, but colonialists avoid customs, by checking charts containing African cattle crossing captions. Anyhow all being briefed beforehand, come carrying critical chapter about Chad, absolutely critical as always, as August advances, colonialists break a couple bones, and being concerned about assuming control, cut all avenues, cut banana crop, cut cables and capture captivating Afrikanische Ameisen. After another crossing colonialists change currency, change certain complex conduits, creating a concern among captured Chadians . . . come, come, always complaining about colonialists changing African air. Aiii. Cut.

As always, Chester amuses Alva by continuously casting aspersions against crazy Alex and corpulent Allen, and also casting Corinthian carvings against Alva's bedroom ceiling. Anyhow, all consider Chester a bloody bore . . . At Chester's Chad college, a couple, coherent and clean-cut colleagues, citing Chester's Catholic conversion, complain about Chester's aggressive colonialist customs. Chester answers, calling colleagues competitive, also calling colleagues crazy crapulous cretins. Chester also criticizes author's Congolese Cubism chapter as being conservative and anticlassical crap. Congolese cannot create a culture, can barely cook cucumbers, curds and cauliflowers. Colleagues counterattack, cursing current bullshit curriculum, cursing Chester's close-mouthed, chunky, cheap boyfriend. Cheap boyfriend, cheap Chester, cheap chauvinist, cocksucker Chester. Alva claims a cuneiform Cosanostra could cure Chester's Catholic assumptions. But can Alva's claims also cure Americans bombing Chad beaches. Anyhow, all concur America's angst cannot corrupt Chadians.

Arriving at Chad, Alex and Allen coldly consider childlike Chad attitudes, and calculate, can Chadians afford American cosmetics.

American army colonel apologizes about bombing beaches, claiming acid-carrying aviator blew all aeronautic bombing controls. Anyhow, assures Chad, bombs are clean as August breeze.

Cut buffoonery, cut Alva's bleached-blonde bisexuality, add Chad cowboys, buffaloes, also Bantu clobbering cheap Chester, also create an additional African army, adding another catastrophic anthill collapse as army advances, courage, courage, as birds chirp; biu, biu, biu, Ahhh . . . Contentment.

African confessions are a bit bloated, a bit bloodied, a bit comical, as all causality and awareness cannot cure a common cold.

At Chad's costume club and boutique, called after Alva, an anthropologist carefully applies American cosmetics, cajoling customers, come baby, come baby, afterward counting classic buck. Close chapter.

6

D

DISPUTING DENSE CONFUSION about campaign
aims, Dogon army accepts a cuneiform dogma, accepts a cen-
tralized demolition blast, but didactic campaign aims are
alarming all alligators, ants and antelopes, although Dogon
colonel admiringly claims bombs are acting as deodorants.
Bombs can also clean bush and beaches, an absurd assertion,
and dress cities, and convince Africans. Demonstrably, cuneiform
devices can decode Africa's dangerous demography, and also describe Alva and Albert desultorily crossing desert, drinking
Dogon beer, and complaining a bit about dehydration, both asking: Can determination conquer despondency. Asking: can an
ant covet another ant. As another day breaks, both, dawdling a
bit, come closer and closer, altogether a curious case, as both
alternately carry a box containing a cuneiform dictionary
and a cuneiform code and directions. Albert deceives Alva
by describing Dogon antiquities as being Chadian. Double
dumb Alva, doesn't dispute Albert. During crossing Albert
comes across an ancient discarded dictaphone, and dictates a
definitely desirable description all about a circumscribed desert
city, but being Albert, city's a bit derivative. Albert downcast
and disconcerted because Alva claims beautiful desert architecture defies description.

Arriving at Dogon, both desperately desire a drink, and a
bite, anything, as affable citizens bring dishes. After a bit both
are delicately chewing choice Dogon duckling and Chad dump-

7

ling, as dumbstruck Dogon citizens brave actual bombs, defying air attacks, applauding Alva, applauding digestive drama. Admittedly Alva's curvaceous bare breasts and bare belly are an additional attraction, but all, also dig Albert's angst. As an archeologist Albert admits digging decay. Dumb Albert, distance doesn't deliver dental degrees. Distance delivers death.

Can a destitute country augment a broadly based dictatorship by adding cosmetic counters, asks author after changing Alva's beach apartment and becoming dress because colors clash. Consider, anyone claiming cosmetics can color beaches, could cause a constitutional crisis, argues Albert after converting another bomb crater, and creating a cosmetic bargain basement.

At daybreak, an African army captain attends a Bach concert at an army camp. As always bugler cautiously blows Bach, beautiful Bach, as an army captain, citing duty, calmly cuts down drummer, chopping at arms, at body, also cutting down bugler, clean convenient cuts, and dismembering a dozen conductors, all crawling among ants, all dreading clean convenient cuts. Capricious Alva complains African amusements are a bore. As another chapter closes, contradictions appear and are described by author as defining another childhood, an agreeable childhood. Author concludes as carefree bearded aviators comb beaches, admire Dogon architecture, chase ants, admire African bare beauty, drop acid at bazaar, drop bombs, crossing desert, digging antiquities, and all consecutive A.D. and B.C. dates. Ahhh.

As Alva's date blows Bach's baroque bugles, Alva deliriously awaits delicious changes, and also admits, ages ago Alex asked: Do . . . ? Definitely, answered Alva. Again Alex asked: Did . . . ? Definitely. Alva's autobiography describes another allegorical character. Dumb bastards didn't . . . couldn't . . .

Anyhow Alva conspired against both Alex and Allen, but both don't deserve a complete chapter.

African armies consider buying American draft beer. Beautiful brew, also consider denouncing another dictator, as Congo's current dick, Duizinan, attends a ceremony at a captured air base, bashfully accepting canvas diploma containing cash, and a Burundi cane chair, afterward Duizinan applauds as boys choir chants an appropriate anthem. Ahhh beautiful.

Alva's autobiography consummately describes Duizinan's awkward caresses, Duizinan's cleft chin, and captivating chubby cheeks, Duizinan's cheap collapsible couch and dark damask drapes, and cautious attendants carrying bows and arrows and Duizinan's black convertible Cadillacs, all classical devices, as Duizinan captivated by Alva, advances, complaining a bit, after all aging Duizinan cannot . . . despite . . . because . . . as attendants, drawing bows and arrows, clamor, careful . . . dangerous. . . . Duizinan dies. Can Alva's account be correct?

Designing African canals again brings bright changes: brings drowning cows, drowning antelopes, alligators, deer and ants. Another colossal catastrophy. Alva's bare breasts droop, as Chester's alarming deafness darkens African continent, and all despair because Chester cannot hear Dogon birds chirp: biu, biu, biu, or Dogon dogs bark: bow, bow, bow, or antelopes: blit, blit, but Chester can dream and draw beautiful dandelions blooming against an African countryside, as defiant Dogon divisions advance against anthills, capturing Dogon bush and dust, creating dangerous canals, designing Africa again and again.

Chester alone, dreams: Alva disrobing, displaying body, displaying curvaceous breasts. All dreams culminate in dramatic deeds.

9

E

ENOUGH. Alva accidentally encounters an Ethiopian engineer bearing dandelions, but decides engineer's action entails an enormous and energetic eagerness at both elbows. Ethiopian engineer cries, don't, as Alva, eluding elongated Ethiopian arms, escapes, despite certain beautiful architectural details. Emitting English entreaties, engineer collides against closing elevator door, almost admitting defeat, engineer considers all angles, all apertures, all doors, and deduces correctly another beginning and another end. Encountering Alva's elbows at a basement college cafeteria, he detects Alva close by, but again Alva changes costumes, escaping disguised as a Corinthian column. Eventually chase ends at airport. Alva enroute eating edible escargot, delicious, but after departure all eight engines begin dripping, evicting evil evidence, Ahhh, bother, bloody burdensome bother. As another August day closes, a distraught engineer bangs dishes against counter at airport, bloody ass, demanding everyone's attention, exhibiting effeminate English errors by behaving badly. As engines continue dripping, airborne Alva coolly applies airforce experience, exchanging all engines, and excitedly exclaiming: Eritrea exists, Eritrea exists.

Enough.

Eight engines can easily energize Ethiopian capital. Even

10

Emperor admires competence, and after examining Alva's allegorical chapter concerning certain climactic encounters, enlists engineer's assistance. Easily accomplished. After Alva's departure engineer entertains Edna at Dropsy's. Delicate English Edna, emulating Alva, approaches all covert couriers a bit eagerly. Easily done, engineer advises Emperor. Afterward Emperor erroneously calls Edna, Alva, and also Dearest Damsel. Entices Edna, alias Alva, and copying engineer's example also entertains at Dropsy's, eying Edna's easy elipsoid boundaries. Ahh, as above all eight ear-splitting engines energize Empire. But Empire crumbling. Elatedly Emperor enters Edna believing Edna could be Alva, as Edna, a bit deferentially, a bit dishonestly admits coming eight consecutive colossal and definitely contagious climaxes. Afterward, Edna admits being Edna. Dismayed Emperor conceals drooping erection. Edna? Dearest Damsel. Demure damsel eagerly clutches at Emperor's defenses, but Emperor, deeply embarrassed, draws back, coughing, a bit calculatedly, cough, cough, but by coughing Emperor accidentally creates a complex code designed by bombing consultant. As Emperor considers balling Edna again, airplane erroneously bombs beleaguered Ethiopian capital, eliminating everything below. Capital becomes antiquity dated A.D. Afterward, eager engineer espouses discarded Edna, becoming engaged, entwined, entrenched, estimating Edna's capabilities, either eight boys, eighteen boys, eighty boys, enough, enough.

Erasing Eritrea, erasing Ethiopia.
Easy come, easy . . .

Alex and Allen deny Antibes, deny everything.

F

FERDINAND, another African freak, flies Eastern frequently, first class, forgetting close family connections, father, aunts, cousins, forgetting French flag, forgetting everything but decadent French entrees, fried frogs, for example, and French entertainments and French cosmetics. At Funtua Ferdinand comes across four fresh Fulani female florists feverishly demonstrating forbidden fly-by-night festivities for Ferdinand's benefit. Fantastic Africa . . . Clearly Ferdinand, carrying cosmetic case, carrying French cash, feels African entrapment, feels dubious excitement, four females, but Ferdinand betrays a certain alarm, and finds excuses, a bit fatigued, a bit drowsy, a bit drunk, also full from eating entrees. But four females form exquisite embraces, as Ferdinand forgetting appointments, forgetting cosmetics, advances, following archetypal advice, embracing an African atavism, African boundaries. Forward, Ferdinand. Fabulous Fulani figures crouch, fabulous fucks, as Ferdinand's fingers feel fragile-boned Fulani frames. Forward. Ferdinand eagerly follows fantastic fragrance, follows fabulous fullness. Forward. But female florists frustrate Ferdinand, forming a circle all embrace among flowery but cheap bedding, forsaking fastidious Ferdinand, a future cosmetician, forsaking Ferdinand and fucking bedroom furniture. Chairs first, flowered Bantu cane chairs. Downcast, feeling dejected after first frustrating African experience, Ferdinand flies back. Flies first class Eastern. Enjoys fried frogs for dinner. Fabulous dinner. Fabulous frogs, author decides. But erases Ferdinand. Feeble fucker.

Establishing an African dictionary about certain favorite Fulani fetishes, author arrives at five, feeling fine, although a bit forsaken, but fine enough . . . Everywhere broad avenues, clear autumn day, bright black faces applauding, cheering, but few female florists among audience. Author a bit disheartened. Feeling conspicuous as a foreigner, also feeling everyone else can freely express a certain common denominator, a denominator excluding author. Africa advertises, broad daylight forever. Eastern Airlines advertise, five fetish flights.

Africa again: discount furniture, a bit drab but colorful, broad avenues built along French design, also exotic flowers, and a few Fulanis feverishly clapping, creating a confusing atmosphere. A festive climate, admits an Eastern Airlines clerk. A copybook design for a dictionary, author decides. Bedroom faces east, faces city dump, called "Famous Fabala Abyss." Congenial bookstore close by, but desk clerk blocks exit, demanding a fifty-dollar advance.

Filming above action for advertisement, Eastern executive decides fetishes can be fun, but Eastern fires director after appalling balling between frogs carried by airline for first class dinner. Enough.

Ferdinand flies back, discovers France, embraces flag, father and aunts. Ahhh, Flaubert, Céline, Balzac. Disgusted author eliminates Ferdinand.

13

G

GENUINE GESTURES are African gestures, because Africans can by a few gestures demonstrate a deep and abiding affection between altogether different foreign bodies, each clap, each groan, each facial gesture conveying a convincingly eternal dramatic African confusion and also a fusion of bodies, as bodies explore boundaries, generously emitting a fresh African ecstasy, and by bringing gifts, following each day's example, as each day brings certain gifts, all Africans drop bows and arrows and closely embrace an anticipation. Correspondingly, author asserts, a boundary cannot collapse before all appropriate gifts are delivered. Accordingly, France, Germany, America deliver gifts.

Ghanaians are erroneously convinced German gestures can cut floods, can cook beetles, can deafen Africans, but German gestures are all futile, besides being enormously funny.

Gustaf's gastronomical gladness cannot conceal Gustaf's bloated belly, Germany's generals gloomily admit as gifted Gustaf entertains Alva at Gabon's best diner. Good Gabon food. But everyone at diner genuinely alarmed by German's great girth, by German's great appetite. Gobbling gestopfte Gans, gobbling Gabelfrühstück, gobbling goulash, gobbling Geschwind, Gesundheit, Gesundheit, gobbling Gurken, Guggelhupf,

14

Gash Gash, Gish Gish, groaning, grunting, also complaining, chewing Grune Bohnen, Geschmacksache, as Germany grows greater. Alarmed, Gabon grows additional food for Gustaf, and Gustaf's children, Gerda, Grete and Gerhart. Gifted Grösseres Germany consumes energy and guarantees greatness, get going, grow another Goethe, great guy, claims Gustaf, as all Grundig gramophones in Gabon, gently croon: Goethe, Goethe, Goethe.

Are Germans convincing in Africa? A glowing G-man arrives, gripping black gloves, bearing a granite chin, cheerfully granting Germany a concession. After checking culinary boundaries, Gustaf eats a dozen breakfasts and dinners, and also assists Gabon airforce. Admits aviators are ganz gute Burschen. Also Gabon ganz gemütlich: broad avenues built along French design, also a few bars and boutiques, fortunately Gabon bush "ganz echt Afrika."

Back at Angola, Alex and Allen are buying an expensive chart containing clear directions for finding certain gold amulets. Chart covers four acres. Contemplating chart both are attacked by African ants, forgetting gold amulets and Alva, both flee following African army's flight also from a determined attack by fierce ants. Author despairs. Abandoned chart carried away by ants. Alex calls Allen: a fucking ant fleeing coward.

H

HIS HOPES have had a disastrous effect, Alex admits, having handicapped Alva and her femininity, having frustrated her femininity, and her desire for a better art education, and a desire for better fucks, because after all Allen had always been home, had always been around, holding both back from coming closer and closer, consequently, his and her frustrated hopes have also handicapped Africa, because both, by being around, by buying a few guns, and a few gold coins, and have held Africa back from coming closer and closer and closer, both forward and backward, as a continent, as a huge bank account, and as a bird cage. How can Africa attain all heavenly hopes, as all exotic birds chirp: biu, biu . . . Even a certain foreign diplomat conceded, Alva's fantastic frustrations about Alex have dashed all African hopes for future fucks, her hopes and Alex's hopes are continuously competing, continuously clashing. Every African feels her disorientation, feels her grave feminine discontent, as Alva gazes at *Harper's Bazaar,* gazes at glossy designs beyond her attainment . . . as bewildered Africans, after chasing a few ants, come back and follow Alva's gaze, disconcerted by foreign ceremonies, by complicated foreign coupling and frenzied copulation and disturbing competition between Alex, Allen and Alva, as another coveted bush coat comes apart, diminishing every hunter's hopes. Allen forever explaining: hunter's hopes are alien, even a bit absurd for Africans, because hunters come here for hunting Africans. Actually, even Alva's harmless hopes can disillusion any African army hurtling forward, crushing grass and ants, drinking coconuts, and being clobbered by foreign airplanes. But Alva's enthusiastic German, her Herman, enjoys African dangers, enjoys digging holes, holes house hope . . . as Africans acknowledge a cuneiform discipline, a bit chaotic and formless but awfully correct, however chaos doesn't deter Herman from clobbering his cook for burning his goulash.

Alex and Allen haven't got an engineering degree, haven't come here for airport construction, or contemplation, or free African amusements. But each feels hopeful about Africa, and crossing Africa each feels greater hope. Africa has elephants and circular huts, and dancing chieftains, and complex ceremonies, and a few hunters, how hopeful. Both haven't forgotten Alva, how hopeful. Both hire a guide, how hopeful, how fruitful, but ages ago, Alex admits, he hammered away at Alva's hopes, at her head, how hollow, how humiliating. An alarmed desk clerk complains Alex's blows are cracking a ceiling. Eventually he'll forget, he'll forget because forgetting can be easy, can be hopeful. Allen attempts forgetting an abandoned chart. Hopefully Allen can accomplish full forgetfulness, and forget how he and Alex fled from a few hundred African ants.

Holding a German-African dictionary, Herman acclaims, Die Hoffnung. Blond, cold blue eyes, he boldly claims a few hundred acres for himself, for building bridges and airports, for exploring all African fauna and flora. How hopeful. Admittedly, his dictionary hampers blacks growing barley, corn and cucumbers. All dictionaries hamper black farmers. How does a German express himself. He has a dictionary. Consequently he has a certain hope, and he builds a bridge or an airport for future compulsive explorations. But explorations hamper African festivals. How does a German express himself at a festival. He has a dictionary. Consequently he always has hope and confidence, he can also correct a book, or a husky German female, by calling: heel, heel. But an African? Alas, a German dictionary hampers African contemplation. Also hampers Africans corking bottles. Bottles are Flaschen. Er begreift alles, antwortet der Deutsche. How dull. Her beginner's German hasn't found Herman easygoing. Germans aren't easy. Germans are cautious buyers. Her hopes are dashed by a bedroom dictionary. Her body descends gracefully from Herman's first floor bedroom, and accepts approval, applause, but her head holds an altogether different attitude. How abhorrent a dingy African hotel can be. Having had a boyfriend called Alex and another called Allen and a convertible, an airplane, a hundred Dior dresses, a beautiful beige bag, and antelope boots, and also a carpet, and fantastic breasts, beautiful hands, but hateful fingernails. How honest. He, as an authentic African, approves. He doesn't hesitate. During Herman's absence he flashes his French correspondence course degree, confidentially. He also has a heated expression. He heats her. Each confidingly discloses additional credits, additional cars, dresses, diplomas, hats, boots, estates, French and English. How frightfully extraordinary, he exclaims, hurriedly embracing her. He doesn't have a dictionary, but he can easily comprehend certain external changes. He can also determine Herman's ability behind a gun. Consequently he first fixes Herman, an accident. After a few army friends, all corporals, fix Herman's goulash, he comes back, and dashes about Herman's hotel, closing all doors. One hundred and fifty doors. Feeling a bit fatigued, he falls atop

Herman's bed, but he's heavy and floor collapses. Her considerable expectations are crushed, her floating hopes drowned.

African cinema arouses hope. Dead Herman, how hopeful. An African film director considers casting doors for above action. Do all doors creak, he asks. Crest-fallen because Alva doesn't have enough acting experience, he considers filming Alex and Allen. But both are happy crushing ants, experiencing another childhood and exploring bush.

Actually Angolan history books confirm everything, charts, explorations, discoveries, black bodies, gold. But do both Alex and Allen exist. Angolans exist, bright cloudless day exists, broad avenues, bright flowery costumes and deceptively friendly faces exist. Friendly faces are as abundant as hidden architectural details, dilapidated hotels, dogs, fleas. Afternoon, author drops by at a favorite bar. His hands hold his destiny. He grips an African counter, and conceives another fictional character. Do both Allen and Alex desire Alva? Can desire be an essential entity for a book. He has already eliminated a few emotions. Emotions can be deceptive. Everywhere Africans are applying American cosmetics, hopefully creating bewitching effects.

How about Alva. Her hair hasn't changed. Her eyes are blue-green, her hands hold him. He has a bright Hungarian grin, he chatters a lot, he also has a Hungarian engineering degree. He also has black hair, a fixation about bridges and a completely false confidence. He believes he can blow Bach's bugles, but first he admits he'll build an airport. Each day he delays another formidable event. Each day he asks her,

19

how's everything coming along, baby? He evidently can't handle her desire. But her cosmetic concerns about herself haven't changed. Guinea's forest fires haven't changed drastically either. He greets her effusively. He describes another day's airport construction. He's a fake, Alva decides. A fucking fake.

Alva claims having a husband, as his fake hands encircle her firm breasts. He's disconcerted and annoyed. Her former husband, Alva claims, had completed a dozen airports, and after her departure, has hired a hundred guides, all hunting for her. Even her Hungarian appears a bit doubtful. Alva's claims are a device, a consummate device. His fake hands encircling her breasts are also a device. Are both devices equally effective. But how can Alva consider him?

I HAVEN'T BEEN HERE BEFORE. I had hoped I could hire a car, but I can't drive. I have been awfully busy finishing a book about Alva. First I contemplated doing a book about another character, and another country. Bit by bit I have assembled Africa. Although I hate hot climates I chose Africa. Desire is always alive in hot climates I have been informed. I brought a gun along, and a calendar. It is August here. Bright beautiful August. I used to draw Alva. Her face, her hands, her breasts. But I'm an amateur artist. I didn't bring any drawings along. I am alone. I have a bedroom facing famous Fabala Abyss. I had great hope at first. A great beginning. Imagine. Fabala Abyss. But I discovered it is a city dump. Incidentally, history apparently divides both Allen's and Alex's hunt for Alva into five broad categories. Allegorical, anthropological, bibliographical, geographical and fantastical. All five groups are demonstrably dubious, because all history in Africa is hearsay, and consequently, although Africa indubitably exists, history cannot correct certain highly erroneous assumptions. But history can conceal assumptions. It can confound historians, authors, booksellers, and also doom armies. For instance, each African army is given a few erroneous dates, a few important defeats for discipline, a few false facts, and an arrival and a departure, all contained in a book, a fictional book, but extremely accurate, extremely factual concerning foreign invasions, i.e.

21

bombing beaches, busted branches, better benefits. Also examples: African fusiliers combing hills and forests for Alva, gorgeous Alva, are attacked by Bantus at around five A.M. Impressive, certainly. But all Africans have developed a defense against books. I discover African defense in a hotel bathroom. Dubious history being flushed down a bottomless green hole. Are all armies guided by an author's intuition?

Incidentally I come across another interesting incident. An engineer asks Alex if irrationality isn't implicit in Ibo's imagery. And doesn't it, he asks, illustrate Ibo's continuous illogic. All Ibos, he further claims, have imported illogic, implementing impediments all along, because childish Ibos are grateful for having inherited a gift for innocence. Insatiable Alva arrives in Ibos' country, feeling happy, basking in heat, finding Ibos' innocence appealing. Decorating her hut Alva immediately integrates incomprehensibly advanced Italian construction ideas in Ibos' instinctive intentions. How ideal. How decorative. Alva installs inlaid ivory into castiron isometric interiors. Afterward an itchy Italian engineer gravely inspects ironwork, commenting about handiwork, his hands itching for Alva, as he introduces crude comments about irrigation, about flooding gardens . . . Alva is instantly alert, gauging his approach, but concluding it is Italian, and basically buffo.

I have a home, and an attached garage containing an African chart, and a few exotic flowers. I have been accused by good friends, frequently and falsely, as having injured and insulted a former female companion. I deny it. I've had all exotic flowers destroyed, and a collection of butterflies crushed, and a china cabinet broken, because I allegedly insulted and injured a former female companion. Finally I fled. I hope I can

22

finish a book about Alva, but I am being impeded by her feet, by her fleshy calves. I am hungry for her, but her feet are clearly a great impediment. I can't cross her feet. I can't even cross her indifference. I am convinced her indifference is a device. I have fled carrying a few African carved figurines, hoping I could finish book, instead I encounter immense African boredom. I feel African boredom houses a gigantic floral bouquet. It is immense, it is as broad as all avenues in eastern Guinea combined. Both African boredom and her feet are forbidding impediments I hadn't anticipated at all.

Everywhere I go I come across engineers constructing Africa. Almost all have balled Alva in between building a few bridges. For instance, an Italian brought her into his hotel. He cannot ignore her exciting breasts and captivating gestures. But how hasty he acted by bringing her into his bedroom. He's in a bind. He's building a dam, he also hunts alligators, antelopes, ants, actually anything, he cheerfully admits. How funny he is, but his childish face doesn't hold her attention. He closes all conduits all hopelessly defective doors. Afterward her casual bye bye confuses his instinctual amorous brain.

Italians are insatiable in bed, asserts an Italian engineer. Italians are also immensely intriguing and inventive. Having invented great art and Eritrea. But inventing another country cannot be accomplished in a day. Inventors drift into inventing almost dreamily, almost by accident. For example, I came here, dreading heat, dreading ants, dreading bush fires, and being hit by a hurtling elephant. After arriving I immediately build a few defenses, I avoid enticements, I avoid African ceremonies, and I avoid being challenged by a gun-carrying hunter.

23

I contemplate crossing Africa in a book: it is a familiar book, and it contains a familiar army, a couple of ex-convicts, a former colonel in British intelligence, also a Graham Greene admirer, and Alva, but her hands and feet impede as I hurl invective at her, like fresh divisions into battle. In chapter eight an Angolan or Ibo army is advancing against a defiant and confident adversary. It advances, even as it is being decimated, it advances biting bullets, eating dust, and hitting antelopes, alligators and ants. But how hopeless. How hysterical. A few German captains guide an African division. Gute Burschen, hopla, hopla. As a group Germans eat differently from Africans. However each claps in an African fashion. Also hops about a bit awkwardly, feeling a bit absurd. I anticipated everything, absolutely everything. If I ever encounter Alva I'll apologize for insulting her.

J

JUST JOURNALS? Just confessions? Alex's chief indiscretions are his collected journals. He carefully chose black cowhide covers because black isn't conspicuous. He carries his journals in a battered bulky brown cowhide briefcase, a gift from Alva. Invariably he hides his journals in his bedroom. He conceals his journals from Allen's eyes. His journals are in effect a documentary evidence, justifying his journeys. Indeed, Alex justifies himself by jotting down in his journals everything he does. If he hides his bulky journals from Allen, it is because he is hiding himself. He has considered hiding himself, but he is heavy and consequently hiding himself isn't advisable, isn't even feasible. Instead he hides all evidence of his feelings concerning Alva, Allen and himself. Daily he industriously edits and deletes and also adds a few items concerning his appetite, his intentions, his interest in his African guide and Allen's curious jealousy. But basically he is describing his journal and his journeys in his journal. He explains it as follows: it is a journal about a journey from Jader, and another journal about a journey from Jebba. Jader and Jebba are far apart. Few Africans have been in both cities, because few can cover a great distance by foot. Alex has jotted down each day's distance in his journal, because accuracy is essential, because he can hide his intentions from Allen behind an incredibly detailed account, an in-depth account including exact distances. But Allen isn't curious. Anyhow, in Africa black-covered journals are common, I discover, among foreigners. I can easily cite a dozen examples. A few are influenced initially by a desire for an acceptable and dignified hobby. But hobbies form habits. André Gide had a journal. It influenced his habits. He also hid his journals in his bedroom as long as he could. But Gide hadn't been in Jader and Jebba. As for Alex, his journals contain his insight into Allen's bizarre conduct, into Allen's apathy, into Allen's easygoing cheerful acceptance of Africa. Alex describes his astonishment. How can Allen accept Africa. Actually, Alex's descriptions and his concern aren't about Allen at all. Alex is chiefly concerned about his discovering his inacceptable darkness. Each journey is an excuse for exploring his despondency, consequently his journals are false. If Allen isn't curious about Alex's journals it is because he is clever, and because if one compares both Allen's and Alex's heads he has a better head. Alex continuously carries his heavy and false journals in his briefcase. Because his journals are exceedingly heavy, he doesn't carry anything else. His bags are being carried by an African guide. In his journals Alex also explores his guide's joviality. But his chief concern is his journals. His journals are actually a joint exploration, a combined journey, he and his guide having joined forces, despite Allen's anger. Alex classifies everything he encounters in a clinical fashion: I believe I dislike Allen. Because he is a creep. Because he isn't clean. Because he isn't curious. Because he doesn't care about Africa. Because he can fall asleep during an African ceremony. I can cover five hundred feet in half an hour. I can endure Alva's anger, but I cannot endure Allen's bad breath.

I don't care if Allen and Alex are in Africa, I don't care if both are hunting for Alva, because I am. I am. And I have an accurate chart, and a dictionary and her description.

26

KNOWING KANT INTIMATELY helps, as I keep a clear head. I'm fascinated by Alex and Allen going back and forth. I can infer from Alex's journal both his and Allen's intentions. Both are killers. Both came here because killing is easier in Africa. Both have had a certain experience in common. I know Alex is extremely irritated because his guide is also keeping a journal. Alex claims Africans cannot keep elegant journals. He contemplates killing his guide, just as he has contemplated killing Alva. I don't know how he intends to do it. Everything is elusive, Alex complains. Both in Jader and Jebba he came across a few good charts, and a few journals containing hand-drawn illustrations depicting him and Allen, carrying guns, crossing fields, carrying journals, hunting for Alva, because Alva knows about a kidnapping in Antibes, but I am getting carried away by coincidental encounters.

Alex can express himself in five click dialects, his knowledge has come in handy, he explains in his journal. He could barter an elephant for a canoe (but doesn't), he could design a new colony (but doesn't), he could also drop Allen (but doesn't), he could comb his hair (but doesn't), hire another guide, buy another black-covered journal, correct a few false facts, assert he's happy (frequently), and have his guide guide him from Jebba and Jader, and from Kapanga and from Kikuyu's fertile foothills. Everything is a challenge for Alex. Alva

27

also had been a challenge. If challenged Alex can kill an African easily, build a house and deep-fry an elephant. If challenged by anyone, he can climb Kilimanjaro (but doesn't), grow grapes for a change or dig for African antiquities (he doesn't). Alex is anticipating a challenge from Allen. But Allen complains, everything is alike: broad avenues, green ditches, grasshoppers, a few ivory collectors, a few apartment buildings, but everywhere a bareness, a desolate bareness, despite contradictory evidence in certain books about Africa.

L

LOSING HER HEAD Alva came here. Being an accomplice in a kidnapping, Alva left in a hurry, left both boys, Alex and Allen, and a body, a kidnapped body. Alva left a long letter, explaining her departure, and leaving Alex all her bills, having just bought a dozen lovely Dior dresses, and antelope boots. Although both lost confidence in kidnapping, both could gladly have killed Alva, gladly and cheerfully. Decisions, decisions. Alex's African guide, Kosakatse Katewane Katabelle, an African chieftain in disguise, jots down in click language Alex's comments about Alva's betrayal. Kosakatse admires Alex, but also believes Alex dumb for having a female accomplice. Alex confides in him everything he doesn't enter in his journal, but he doesn't know a click equivalent for kidnapping.

I came here although I cannot bear African heat, desert heat, bush heat, body heat. I came here because I had hoped I could be more accurate about Alex and Allen and Alva. I also hire an African guide. I describe Alva, her fantastic legs, her involvement in a kidnapping . . . It is difficult explaining a kidnapping in click. I look at him curiously and ask: Is Alva convincing. Is Alva, Alva?

Luckily all Africans have a language. Arriving in Africa I immediately hear a language I don't comprehend. It is a click language of Africa. It goes: click, click, click, like an empty gun. Being an author, I complain a bit. Everyone laughs, everyone clicks. Everyone enjoys a good joke. Bloody author. Bloody ass. Complaining about click languages, complaining about bathroom facilities. But everyone accepts American Express credit card. I have a bedroom facing Lulumbashi and Lake Leopold, called after Leopold a discoverer. Another Leopold, an inventor, also lived here. I haven't discovered anything. I enjoy a dip in it. If I discover a lake I'll call it Alva.

After killing a guy in Antibes, Alex leaves his apartment in a hurry. At first he and his buddy are a bit lost. All charts are confusing. Both haven't got any experience, except for a kidnapping job. Both are looking for Alva because Alex claims Alva emptied a kidnapped jeweler's briefcase before leaving his apartment, and leaving a dead jeweler behind. Alex believes looking for Alva isn't a challenge, it is a lesson in love. He doesn't find Alva, but instead he finds a lot of lakes, and elephant grass and dying antelopes and howling animals, and confusing confrontations between enemy armies guided by Germans, and everyone communicating in a click language. Every guide Alex and Allen hire has known Gide and Conrad, and also Conrad's friend Ford, and Flaubert. All guides are extremely literate and helpful . . . all are imaginative, and for Alex's benefit invent Alva's arrival. It keeps everyone busy. How Alva lived in a jungle. Characteristically, Alva accepts love as it comes. In a jungle, in a hut, in a library. I don't feel jealous anymore. I feel ill. In a book I am finishing I describe how I gave her five hundred dollars. I'm afraid Alva described everything I did in her allegorical autobiography. I have glanced at it briefly. Her daily entries are a bit dreary: I bathed in his lust. He couldn't have enough. He groaned. I bathed again in his lust, in his astonishing desire. I saw in his glazed eyes a fantastic . . . crap, crap, crap. However, I believe Alex is lying. Alva

30

didn't empty a jeweler's briefcase. I believe **Allen** did. Clever Allen. If Alex knew about it he'd kill Allen.

Any lingering doubt Alva ever had is dissolved, is extinquished after her first lover defiantly exclaimed: Kant knows. Bloody bastard. Alva left him. Later, in Africa, being a compulsive liar she lies about him, about Alex and Allen, and about how generous all engineers are. Here, have an airport, have a highway . . . handing her a familiar-looking atlas.

M

MY MEMORY isn't accurate anymore. Mentioning my memory makes me feel insecure. A few months ago Alex and Allen kidnapped a jeweler in Antibes and killed him almost inadvertently. Between eight and eleven A.M. his briefcase containing many fabulous diamonds disappeared from Alex's apartment. My memory concerning his murder is extremely hazy. He appeared to have been a middle-aged man. He had gone to a hotel. Half an hour later he left, and disappeared. His empty car is later found miles from his home. Everyone mentioned his murder before it even happened. I had met him months before at a dinner. He had a few drinks, and affably described Africa. He had made a killing here. He had a large house, a family, children and for a jeweler, many curious interests. He had been in Africa for a few months, buying ivory and all kinds of African jewels. Intrigued I listened as he described Africa, mysterious Africa . . . he described meeting adventurers, and living in a Dogon city, and buying amulets from English-educated chieftains, completely corrupt, but highly educated . . . I found him amusing and intriguing. I met him again at another dinner. But I didn't draw any connection between his murder months later and Alva's abrupt departure. Although I had apparently given her his address, and afterward had also introduced him, because Alva kept insisting. I didn't ask her anything. Finally, I gave her five hundred dollars and kissed her good-bye. I don't know how I became involved. I have always been fascinated by Africa. His conversation about Africa intrigued me. I keep jotting down my memories. It all may come in handy. I don't believe I ever actually met Alex or Allen. If Alva had asked me for more money I'd have given it.

N

NOW I AM HERE, in a motel near a jungle. But I am nowhere near Alva and Alex and Allen. But nowhere near is near enough. I am convinced all know about my arrival, and both men know I gave Alva money. Now I am near a bed, and near a bamboo chair. I am not astonished by African interiors. I had expected a more exotic decor. Although I don't care for exotic interiors, I am intrigued by anything exotic, anything different from my house and garage. My house, garage and my life are insured, but I didn't get a cent after Alex and Allen dynamited my car and garage. I'm convinced both did it. Now I am here. My next move is a moment's decision away. Basically Africa doesn't need any inventions, doesn't even need new interpretation. Now I breathe a bit. I may just lie here. Not making any effort, not making any move, not confronting and challenging my "now." I cannot escape my "now." My entire memory is a fleeting gaze into Alva's face. I am afraid of loving her and have invented her lovers, her engineers, but my inventions may, for all I know, be accurate. I haven't got any intuition. I came here at a moment's notice because my book defied completion. It needed local color. Authentic African cries. I measure my deliberate advance into Africa. I measure my concern, my difficulties, my long horseback journeys. I came here carrying a duffel bag containing a compass, a handgun, a few books, a large map, a dictionary, handkerchiefs, condoms, a classical assortment, also an itinerary. I'm in a black country, everything is dark, everything, even all sounds, heavy, dark, beating drums, in my ears even African joyous dancing appears dark and mysterious. Because I am insecure, I'm always looking at my map, and checking my compass. I am here now in Nkongsamba, and can hear drums announcing my arrival. Everyone knows I came carrying a duffel bag containing a compass, a handgun, a few books. It is laughable. Everyone is curious. I can hear drums announcing my exact location in my bedroom. It is a large comfortable bedroom, much like any bedroom elsewhere. A local chieftain is awaiting my arrival at his hut. Is eagerly awaiting my gifts. A few foreign footprints have been found nearby. I'll have a look.

Distances don't drastically alter each fleeting memory. However, distances can hamper me. Each moment is a kind of impermanent and next "now." "Now" is nonfunctional. Now I am looking at my favorite map of another African country, a country far away from here. Looking at it my "now" is negated, is nullified by my hopes at encountering her. Now, no matter how I hold my map, my location hasn't changed. Finally, in despair, I go downstairs and am greeted by a jazz band, by drums, by feathered hats, by joyous gestures, by incredibly distorted facial grimaces, by more feverish drum beats, and hasty click language communications, and an alluring nakedness, and by breakfast and cheering because I have enriched everyone by bringing my few belongings here. I am inventing another country and another "now" for my book. It is largely an African country, dark, lush, hot, green and inhabited by a multitude of giant ants. But even invented countries follow a common need, as each country heads for a common memory, a common destiny, a common materiality.

Most newspapers in Antibes carried details about a missing

35

case containing a few hundred diamonds, and about a five-foot-eight jeweler named Nicholas, now dead. Killed. An eight-inch knife in his chest. I don't know how Nicholas became a jeweler. He married, had children, a large house in Antibes, another house in Arles, another house, bought as an investment, in Nigeria. He also bought a dog, a few cars and a handgun. Each day he drove from his house. Each day his dog barked as he drove away. He wore a coat, a hat and gloves. He didn't exactly look like a jeweler. He looked more like an African hunter. His appearance excited his customers, and also aroused most females he had known. Every day he met his dubious friends, his business colleagues, and between five and eight, his mistress. He also expressed a great interest in meeting Alva alone, after I had brought her along. I and Alva had dropped in after lunch, for a look at his fabulous ivory collection. He hadn't been in Africa for nothing. He had an adventurous nose. He could discern in her a certain availability. But I didn't dream he'd be murdered merely because I introduced her. Alex and Allen arranged everything, almost making me an accomplice.

OBVIOUSLY Africa's mind cannot be affected by my arrival. Africa's mind is justifiably obstinate about its dislike of all foreign occupation of its land. I'll be here off and on, I explain. I may even go for an occasional drive into a jungle. As of now I occupy a hotel in Otavi. I don't know how everyone behaved before my arrival. Our hotel has a collapsible floor and can be moved in a matter of minutes across Ovamboland. I explained I didn't have any objections if moving it became necessary. My occupation is essentially and necessarily a hazardous one. I have been nearly killed by friends and by enemies. I have lost a garage, a Chevy and a couple of azalea bushes. Admittedly I envied Nicholas, and consequently, having offered him Alva, I must have desired his death. At our first encounter, I didn't observe him carefully. He described Otavi, he described living among blacks near a forest, and later, confidentially, he also described his current mistress. I had a house, I explained, a garage, a car, a couple of azalea bushes but no mistress. I had one in mind, but . . . I hesitated as he laughed. I must admit I liked him, but I also detested myself for liking him.

Most of my maps are old and misleading. Most of my maps are covered by Nicholas's handwriting, by his fucking and misleading directions. After a long conversation between a number of local chieftains and myself, I am convinced Alva may

37

have been here a few days ago. I have even found one of her footprints in a hut. I have also found other evidence. A dirty bathtub, an old letter bearing her initials and a lipstick.

Once I managed a brief glance at her diary. Just for five minutes during her absence. Her oversexed diary didn't mention me. Didn't mention my name, or my behavior, as if I didn't exist. I hope I can complete my book over here, but I keep being distracted by naked black bodies in my bedroom, by gold ornaments and by everyone giggling maniacally. Now I have a cold. Don't mention it again, or I may drop everything. I arrived a few days ago. Following my instinct I came over here. I may leave after I have explored Alva's next move. By now I can communicate in click language. I drink a bit, eat a bit, in between jotting down all kinds of information about life in general, life as it is being lived over here. Because I am heavy, I have to buy a larger car, and I oversleep in a bigger bed. In Ovamboland a librarian asked me for an autographed copy of my book. As fast as I finish it, I promise her. I asked if anyone lately had looked at my collected oeuvres. A collection of my oeuvres in morocco leather is also available, I am informed. By now, all literate Africans are avidly following my oeuvres, my overt oeuvres in Ovamboland, available in fifteen click languages.

Nicholas came here, buying gold ornaments, developing a liking for Africa, for all it offered. Beautiful ornaments, hand-made ornaments, ornaments conveying an ecstasy not known elsewhere, not experienced elsewhere. He'd have come back, if not for Alex and Allen. Instead he died in a bathtub, and all his ornaments, his jewels, have disappeared.

P

PAPER MADE BOOKS POSSIBLE. It also helped prevent illiteracy. I have an interest in books and in paper. An
overwhelming interest, an interest exceeding my interest in
Alva and Alex and Allen. Paper is porous. I freely admit, paper has its defects, its drawbacks. Dipped in a lake it may
disintegrate. I'm on a paper chase. A lovely old English paper
chase, only it's in darkest Africa. Paper is essential for me. But
Africa has existed for centuries independent of paper. It
makes one ponder. Africa also makes me perspire. I had
hoped I could avoid Africa because I perspire easily. I arrived
in Pandamantenga, almost out of paper. After landing I made
hasty inquiries about buying paper. African paper is extremely
porous. It has faint blue lines and Africa's outlines marked on
each page. I don't mind. Africa's paper is produced by pygmies.
It is made from pressed green cucumbers. Long green cucumbers. However, most Africans, a proud and ancient people,
prefer pressed bark cloth. I didn't care for it. I believe it could
constrain a prolific author like myself. But by and large, Africa's
black bourgeoisie looks down on African products, preferring
imported paper, perfume and Pucci boots from Italy. Italians
also are a proud and ancient people. I'm not particularly proud.
I am living in a hotel in Pandamantenga. I have a bit of cash I
intend investing in paper, and maybe one day I'll also be proud.
I have hired fourteen local investigators, part-time only, on a per

39

diem basis. Per diem doesn't exist in any click language. My fourteen investigators are all eager for an assignment. All ask for descriptions, hints, indication of Alva's presence. I can only offer each my collected oeuvres, but not in morocco leather. I lend each one a paperback copy. Peruse it carefully. It contains everything I know about life. My investigators complain it is confusing . . . it is contradictory . . . it is full of hot air. Exactly, I explain. It'll help, because Alva is contradictory, and confusing, and full of hot air. Each, before leaving on his assignment, punches me in a friendly kind of manner. It is painless, but I collapse after five blows.

Africa is changing daily. I'm aware of it changing. Plants and people. Everything around me is changing except my photograph in my passport. It is always accurate of course. It has helped me cross borders and boundaries and overcome all kinds of obstacles put in my path, partly because I am an author, and authors aren't especially popular, and partly because I am engaged in documenting my pursuit of Alva, and consequently I am also inadvertently documenting Africa's constant changes. In general authors are provided a certain liberty. I'm no exception, as everyone happily gives me a certain freedom, and anticipates fabulous distortions. But Africa is not my invention by any means. I have not made any concessions, I have not invented anything I've seen or done. My father is an inventor. He may even have had a part in Africa's changes, indirectly, of course. His box of land changes is immensely popular here. One particular box can drain a lake of approximately one mile in diameter. A couple of Belgian men outside, a nice bunch of guys, are experimentally draining Lake Albert, merely as a diversion. I now have a bedroom facing a large muddy pit. Most people around here aren't happy about Lake Albert's drainage. Everyone misses its former distinctive beauty. A Belgian defending his action, points out he has a license for draining all African lakes approximately one mile in diameter. He proves it. Everyone curiously examines his document. Belgians have a license for driving a jeep. All are competent drivers. Don't drive fast. Everyone has always correctly assumed Belgians have a license for driving. All also have another license for building a fire in a forest, and another license for hiring a guide, and another license for killing alligators, and another license for keeping a licensed female in a motel. I assume a license exists for everything Belgians do. Following a guide's advice, I apply for a hunting license, a driving license, a boat-building license (just in case), an ivory and gold ornaments export license, a printing license (just in case). I feel much better having a license, although each license costs at least five hundred dollars. In Africa for five hundred dollars one can hire an army for one day, but licenses for armies aren't available a licensing official informs me.

Q

QUESTIONS. Questions. I am convinced that people in Africa had been asked questions before I came here. Even in a jungle, questions are commonplace. Merely asking a question did not astonish anyone. In my day I have been asked a great many questions about my books, my life, my house, my car. Everything I did evoked a great many questions. But I haven't learnt much from questions, possibly because I concentrated on my questioner instead of on all questionable questions. But pursuing Alva, questions come in handy. In questioning people, I occasionally forget one question and promptly introduce another. People everywhere are always being asked questions, and almost always obediently answer. I now know much more about Africa, about draining lakes, about dynamiting bridges, but quantitatively and qualitatively my quest for Alva is being impeded. It is impeded by a great many false clues left in motels. It is being impeded by long legs, all looking like Alva's lovely legs, by kneecaps looking like Alva's lovely kneecaps. Daily, out of necessity, I examine a great many lovely legs and kneecaps. Most ladies obediently permit me, possibly even encourage me, as I, ladida, fiddle around, as I consider if a certain kneecap could be Alva's. I long for Alva's perfect knees, perfect ankles, perfect elbows. I handed her five hundred dollars and didn't ask any questions, although I could have. I didn't feel any jealousy, I had my book, my friends, my maps, my pets, my car and my future. Alva knew I had a book about her in mind. I kept jotting down everything Alva mentioned: Alex, Allen and Quat. I must admit, Alex and Allen confused me. I couldn't be certain about both because both, Alva admitted, knocked her about, kicked her occasionally, but not Quat. I also jotted down his description: cocky, cheerful, handsome, alert, bright and black. An endearing man, possessing an eye for a beautiful kneecap, of course. Quat never confided in me, but I'm certain he's here. His African hunter's hat is a dead giveaway. I mentioned him in my books, and questioned all my new black bourgeois friends. But all are embarrassed by my questions, and gracefully cover a quick giggle by placing an immense black palm over a parted mouth. Finally, one day, a hot August day, a man living near Quala'en Nahl had pity on me. For one hundred dollars he gave me a hand-drawn chart and directions enabling me, and my caravan of fourteen camels, and my five jeeps, and my baby elephant and my hired investigators, and my . . . I don't quite know how he put it, but he put it eloquently in click language. He pointed one long finger in a northerly direction. Quat is an African queen, he explained. Queen Quat lives in a flat country north of here, a country painted orange all over. I set off immediately. Finally, my quest is paying off. My questions are paying off. My money is paying off.

R

READING MY BOOKS afterward, reading my collected oeuvres, I can't find any description of my fear, and of my excitement as I chose a road not marked on my map. Reading my old newspaper clippings, I fear for Alva's life, because both are remorseless killers, both are ruthless and relentless bastards, and both have come here for one purpose only. Revenge. Queen Quat isn't mentioned in my old newspaper clippings. Her name has been omitted. Quat's an old hand at being omitted. Queen Quat is roughly my age, and reasonably content, from all I hear, possessing a couple of air-conditioned palaces, a flat country, a loyal people, a public library containing my collected oeuvres. Quat doesn't mind African dishes. He's not a German. He doesn't even mind irritating noises at night. His ears are not as large as mine. His needs are also different. But he also loved Alva. He exists in my book. Occasionally I make a mistake and change his gender. I have given him another name. But of course he doesn't know it. He much prefers Quat. Queen Quat. An African Queen.

Quat, like Alex and Allen in my book, hasn't forgotten Alva. He also may have followed her here, although he may have come for a different reason. I assume he came because of her. But once in Africa, like most foreigners, he began exploiting Africa. He probably got a number of licenses for draining lakes, building bridges, removing mountains, flattening forests for better drainage. He also got an importer's license, importing cosmetics. Africa is a colorful country. People paint designs on each others bodies. Quat arrives looking like a queen, like an advertisement for cosmetics. Looking at him all African reason breaks down. He reminds everyone of a familiar ritual. But he isn't painted enough. At any rate, Africans intuitively comprehend all kinds of ceremonial gestures. Even black bourgeoisie almost always opens its painted doors and acts quite deferentially.

I feel a bit confused. Had Alva lied about Quat. Had her descriptions been false. Has Quat read my books, my collected oeuvres. He may have bought a few in Runbek, a godforsaken hole fifty miles from his palace. He may have read each one of my books, recognizing in every face a familiar resemblance, recognizing Alva. I know Alva had made fun of me, had described me and had encouraged Quat's impersonations of me . . . both played many games. He'd impersonate Africans in bush, and me, mimicking my accent, my awkward embraces, my hesitations. Mimicking my introduction of Nicholas, mimicking my inept plans for acquiring a briefcase containing a fortune in diamonds.

Now Quat is in Africa. He has many influential friends. He has a Cadillac, an airforce and a flotilla of boats on a large lake. Occasionally he enjoys a drive into a rain forest. Because he is powerful, everyone has at first concealed his identity from me. Concealing all kinds of evidence as I kept digging into people's pockets, any pocket I'd come across in my peregrinations. But everyone claimed Quat didn't exist. Everyone claimed he is a figment of my imagination.

Quat helped dispose of Nicholas. He had a car. Occasionally friendship can be based on much less. A car isn't a negligible object. It can carry a body. It is comfortable. It is convenient. A car is at home everywhere. Alex claims Alva grabbed all ornaments. I doubt it. I paid her five hundred dollars.

By and large I prefer a 4B pencil as I draw Alva's face from memory. Alva contains a great many hazy memories for me. A paper and pencil can prevent a collapse of certain desirable outlines, of certain guidelines. I keep correcting my drawings of her long legs, her legs apart, gripping my body in a frenzied embrace, but it is difficult to draw from memory. I've had a few hundred copies made of one drawing. It is quite accurate. It is as close as I can possibly get. Every few miles I drop one on a narrow labyrinthian jungle path leading nowhere. Africans in particular have a good memory for details, for legs, for knees. I hope I'll get a response. I've indicated I'll pay a large reward for information concerning Alva. Not necessarily concerning all of Alva, just a detail is enough. I can find her remaining parts. I've had a few diverse leads. Quat is one. Quat right.

Four days later a rebellion breaks out in a rain forest. A few Pygmies are obstreperous. After a bit of rough-and-tumble, I pull out my revolver, aiming it at one little fellow, and everything becomes normal again. But I cannot forget how repugnant it is killing a man. He resembled Quat, only he had been less handsome, and not as large, but honest, courageous, questioning my license, my permit, my five jeeps and fourteen investigators.

S
SUMMARIZING AFRICA: I can speak more freely. I find fewer and fewer impediments. Soon I'll reach my destination. Soon I'll also complete my documentation and my book. Daily Africa is shrinking from extreme heat and fatigue, as rebels in bush battle African armies led by foreigners. Orders are passed in fifteen magnificent click languages. It is no surprise really if most soldiers are missing. After finding one of my drawings in a jungle, a missing soldier nervously swallows sunflower seeds and contemplates future copulation. An endless dream.

In Antibes a murder is solved. But jewel-studded ornaments are not recovered. A particularly distasteful murder, since Nicholas has been carefully dismembered, and stuffed into a dozen old mailbags. Originality doesn't count. Effectiveness counts. Arms, legs, head, dumped all over France, by recklessly driving Quat. Antibes police are still assembling jigsaw puzzle.

Nicholas had showed me his collection of African gold ornaments. Priceless ornaments. He also showed me his house, quite splendid, cars, expensive Italian racer and a German limousine, his mistress, sexy, slim, black dress, kept crossing her legs, kept licking her lips, kept smiling, also his family, standing at my arrival, standing obediently as if for an inspection. Actually rather routine family, children, et cetera. Also mother staying in house, and a cook. Nicholas evidently needed my sympathetic ear. I accompanied him. I screwed his mistress. But I became bored. A certain routine had been introduced into my life. His dog barked as Nicholas left his house, and barked as Nicholas's children left his house for school, and barked as I came. Everything is Nicholas's fault. His intensity, his craving for my attention, for my approval finally succeeded in making me interested. I had a look around his house during his absence. I also fed his dog out of a certain compassion. How can I explain it. His dog became confused, after I spent a couple of hours each day in his bed. Shirley at first seemed hesitant, seemed reluctant, but I convinced her, giving her evidence about her husband's mistress, his meeting Alva . . . I liked his house. His collection of ornaments. His maps. His diaries.

Summarizing Africa. Pygmies are a good example of how everything is shrinking. My study of Africa is predicated on a gradual shrinkage. But black scholars are oblivious of any dwindling or contraction. All are sociologists. All summarize a common discontent by attacking all black bourgeois housewives. She is sitting on a plastic-covered sofa. Her living room is a replica of a palace living room, only on a much smaller scale. Outside is a large garden, and a cucumber patch, also many bicycles. Most have five gears. Evidently it is a prosperous community. Housewife responds if her name is called. Responds also if sexual overtures are made. Responds if doorbell is rung. Responds even more quickly if all happens at once. Doorbell rings. She quickly dusts her furniture, combs her hair, changes her dress and holds a sophisticated magazine in her hand. All black scholars dream about her. Have fantastic fantasies about her, about her doorbell, her magnificent breasts, her base and border, her bed and belt, her bronze jewels and candelabrum, her ceiling ornamentation and chest, her dress and earrings, her embroidery and façade, her fan and footstool, her fountain and furniture, her girdle and gold brocade gloves, her incense box and jewel case, her key and knocker, her mirror frame and molding, her necklace and piano, her pierced openings and processional crucifix, her quiver and sewing machine. A black scholar describes her magnificent sexual imagination, but actually he is describing his own. Most African studies remain inconclusive.

Quat is quite satisfied. He built his cosmetic empire on a shaky and inconclusive study. A housewife's doorbell anticipates his cosmetic exploitation.

Sunday morning Alva paints her fingernails a bright red. She also paints her lips a bright red. I like my fingernails and lips a bright red, she says. But her African admirers remain skeptical. She spends her day studying African illusions, and concealing her own minor defects. Alva only paints small sections of her body, her African lovers complain. She doesn't deserve our love. But despite African encouragements she refrains from painting herself all over.

As a subject Africa doesn't interest her. Her blonde hair still attracts a lot of attention in a jungle. It still stops cars, and causes a general bewilderment. Africans are distracted from Africa's shrinkage. Distracted from future perils, from invasions and mass exterminations. Quat is right.

Added comments: nothing is concealed. Alva's body is functional. A prime minister is staying in her apartment. Nothing in it startles him, because everything he sees is familiar. After all even he owns a few functional possessions himself. She parts her legs and becomes functional. He functions admirably but is distracted by her dusty furniture, her sloppy-looking apartment and her neglected fingernails. Her fingernails give everyone a startling insight into her life. His manly face

49

becomes sad and glum. She is still comparatively free. However, a few letters are still missing, consequently a few prime ministers are still not listed in her appointment book, and a few million Africans are still being disenfranchised.

Situation in Senegal: Hands clutching her soiled suede pocketbook after being raped by Senegalese soldiers, she says: alas, everything I possess beneath my Dior dress is listed in one of fifteen different click dictionaries. Don't bother about me, study a click dictionary instead. Quat right.

T

THEY KEEP GOING round and round in circles, looking
for trinkets. Things are getting tighter, since they both had been
traced to Tchibanga. Each day they leave false clues, false footprints, false directions attached to trees, just in case someone
should follow their circular track. They have rifles, a Land
Rover, a tough guide and a tent for three. Alex complains that
Allen never lends a helping hand. Both are blind to the fantastic
trees, the immense trees towering over them, and the animals in
the trees, and the tiny poisoned darts lodged in the tree trunks,
darts that missed them the last time around. Even killers are capable of a kind of innocence. One thing at a time, stated Alex.
He couldn't decide how they'd get rid of the trinkets once they
got hold of them, and how they'd share them, and how they'd
pay off the guide. And how they'd change their appearance, if
Quat could do it, so could they. They had heard about my arrival
and assumed that Alva and I had together lifted the case containing the trinkets. They couldn't care less about my true concerns,
about books, about Africa, shrinking Africa. Those two fools are
carrying guns and making a lot of noise, enough to startle an entire jungle. Still, it's also part theater, because they can see themselves returning someday to Antibes, both deeply tanned, and
telling everyone at the bar about their trips, their incredible African trips. How they finally found Alva, killed her, and removed
the trinkets . . . at that point their minds stop. Alex carefully
keeps his mind on immediate necessities. He shines his shoes

and also shaves. His mind hasn't hit one blank spot. But he does miss the newspapers. He liked to read about himself.

Tanzania is celebrating the anniversary of Quat's arrival. Everyone is rehearsing for the gigantic tableau. Since's Quat's coronation, no one can quite trust or accept another person's gender. The customs officials have learnt to ask: are all airplane pilots airmale. They're always compulsively touching all those control knobs. They keep on demanding longer and longer runways, says Tiutu, Quat's aide. I land in test tube Tanzania. I have never been in Tanzania before. I have in the course of a long life spent in libraries leafed through a couple of picture books about Tanzania, and also, in my spare time, published a number of authoritative articles about Africa's shrinking land mass. Africa, and that includes Tanzania, is shrinking, at least that is how I presented Africa. It caused no end of a furor. To think that day by day Africa is getting smaller and smaller, less and less significant. Queen Quat of Tanzania personally sat in the airport tower, and taking control of our landing, talked the plane down. Is that a guy or a fucking dame, asked the pilot after he had received his click instructions. A ragged guard of honor greeted me as I stepped off the plane. I had been detained in Nairobi, and arrived three days late. The guard of honor had been standing at attention round the clock for three days (that's how I run things over here, said Quat) and kept collapsing from fatigue and sunstroke. Queen Quat nimbly stepped over their bodies, coming toward me with outstretched hands. All of Tanzania is privy to our embrace. The moment her familiar perfume tickled my nose I started to sneeze. Dear boy, said Quat. Quat doesn't look a day older. Her face breaks into a lovely smile. Everyone around her is relieved. She has quite a temper, explained Tiutu. I too feel relieved, sensing that I had nothing to fear, despite my malicious books, my malicious insinuations.

Life at the palace follows a certain pace, a slow and incredibly boring pace. The Queen, Tiutu explains, the Queen has to take care of a lot of business. There's hardly any time for gaiety. I never mention Alva or the two crooks, Alex and Allen, since I'm afraid of her reaction.

Conforming to the sedentary life at the palace, the people in Tanzania manage to keep themselves occupied. No one is permitted to die of boredom. Quat takes me into her boudoir, and there lets down her hair. Life in Tanzania is predicated on the colored maps of Africa that hang in the palace, courtesy of *National Geographic*. On the maps Tanzania is colored a bright orange. Neighboring Malawi is light blue. The maps are the key to our future prosperity. The maps keep everyone employed, says the Queen. Slipping into a pair of alligator boots, she then proceeds to take me on a tour in her helicopter. From an altitude of five thousand feet everything below, including the city, is a bright orange. Astonishing. I thought it's the effect of the sun. No dear boy. She patted my knee. Each day one hundred thousand Tanzanians carrying ladders, buckets of orange paint and brushes, are driven and also flown to different sections of the country. They paint everything in sight. Since I manufacture acrylic paints, everything needs a frequent going over. It takes about six months to paint this country by hand. She sighs. I suppose there are more efficient methods. But this is by far the most thorough. The Queen also proudly explains that Malawai has also decided to conform to international mapping standards, and since Tanzania had a technological headstart, she could export a light blue paint to Malawi. Angola is another matter entirely. Angola is green on the map, and that may account for their huge relief rolls. I can't, she said, even talk Angola into giving their foliage an extra bit of luster. Returning from the tour, my head is still spinning. All those statistics. At present half a million men are building roads for the painters, the Queen had told me. It'll enable the painters to do their job in half the time.

The next day I asked Quat how she had been crowned Queen. Modestly she said that she had been crowned by the people. She had become so popular. Tiutu put it differently. Queen Quat had disposed of a lot of gold ornaments and invested in a small cosmetic factory. Soon after she opened a paint factory, the first of its kind in Tanzania. Tanzanians admire and respect the Queen. She is so colorful. Indeed, so much had been printed about her. Entire books . . . I sadly agreed. Entire books. Quat right.

The low hills of Tanzania are a bright orange. The people appear happy. All families now possess a long ladder, and that is a certain enrichment. They all store their ladders outside their huts at night. No one seems to be afraid of thieves. At least, not of ladder thieves. If ladders are so readily available, there's no need to protect them. Another deterrent may be the penalty. In fact, over half the men building the roads, and half of the painters, are paying off one penalty or another. Still, I saw no sign of an opposition to the Queen. Not one sign. Not the slightest trace. And it stands to reason that if a people are discontented they form an opposition. How can I speak to the opposition, I asked Tiutu. There's none, he replied simply. The people are happy. During the daylight hours the happy people of Tanzania climb their ladders. But they are lazy, the Queen complains. They have secretly fixed small chairs to the top of their ladders, and now spend hours sitting on top, staring into the blue sky. Of course, one has to punish a few just to set an example. The Queen shrugs her shoulders. In the late afternoon I climb a tall ladder and test the chair I have attached to the top. Not bad. It's quite comfortable. I stare at the sky. At the orange-colored landscape. At the shrinking landscape. Somewhere out there Alex and Allen are desperately driving around in a gigantic circle, blind to everything around them. They too, I suppose, still think the orange glow in the distance is caused by the sun.

U

UNDERNEATH A LARGE ORANGE UMBRELLA, the Queen and I speak of old times. I didn't frequent the gay bars, I didn't even know Alex or Allen, still this doesn't prevent us from speaking about the old times, although our old times are limited to a few encounters, three, maybe four. I'm not certain how many. I met her at Alva's place. But she's not interested in Alva. She keeps stressing the fact that she had been particularly fond of Allen, but that's before Alex. Oh, I agree, Alex is brighter, she said. He'd plan all the jobs. The kidnapping that turned into a farce. They never expected Nicholas to have his entire collection of trinkets on him. Suddenly they had a completely new set of priorities.

Understanding Africa requires patience, and an understanding of at least fifteen click languages, also an understanding of the rapidly growing elephant grass, the tribal relationships, and the cuneiform data banks. I know all about the kidnapping farce. In a sense I am its author. I knew Nicholas's habits, I also knew he'd be carrying the case containing the collection of gold ornaments and jewels. I simply failed to tell Alva about it. The Queen had helped dispose of Nicholas. Allen and Alex had cut up the body. Alva had been sent out to get the mailbags. I had helped her, not knowing how they'd be used.

The following day the Queen holds a press conference under a large orange canopy. It is being done largely, I suspect, in order to impress me. Her uniform is that of a colonel in the

55

Uhlans. Her effeminate gestures brilliantly highlight the ruthlessness of her government. The Queen isn't accustomed to holding press conferences. She rambles on and on. She's repeating everything she told me the day before. She doesn't answer any questions. She just speaks about old times. Since she is speaking in English, everything she says is totally incomprehensible to the assembled press corps. Thank you, gentlemen, says Tiutu, finally, cutting her off just as she started to speak about having recently spoken to Alva. Shit, she cried angrily. Tiutu, don't do that again, d'you hear. Just don't do that again.

I still feel upset by the news conference. If Africa is really shrinking it'll be more and more difficult for Alva to evade Alex and Allen. And both are persistent. Both believe she has the trinkets.

As I leave Tanzania, Tiutu sadly tells me that everything is changing. He's convinced that I'll never again encounter a utopia like the present utopia in Tanzania. Already it is being undermined by the thousands upon thousand of Ugandans illegally entering Tanzania. They are attracted by the glorious orange glow from across the lake, he explains. They see it as a sign from heaven.

But I am an unreliable reporter. I can't be depended upon for exact descriptions and details. Even Alva, to her chagrin, discovered that. I have distorted so much, concealed so much, forgotten so much. But I have discovered that people are patient. They say about me: He has a longing. He is still uncovering Africa. He has a certain talent for that sort of task. They also examine everything I publish for evidence of my love for Alva, simply because I said somewhere that it exists. For no other reason. They are understanding. They comprehend love, the shrinkage of an immense continent, and utopias, because they are familiar.

56

V

VEILED THREATS. Prior to my departure, my hasty and unplanned-for departure from Antibes, I kept receiving veiled threats. Sometimes I also received muffled threats. Different male voices on the phone, day and night, explicitly informing me that I had insulted a female member of their family. That I'd better get out of their neighborhood, and abandon my furniture, my house, my garage, my books. I suspected Alex and Allen. But I had no proof. One August day two men burst into my house. They too claimed I had insulted or injured a female member of their family. It's preposterous. Still, I managed to escape. All this is preventing me from finishing my book. The day someone put a stick of dynamite in my car, blowing it and my garage sky high, I threw a few things into a suitcase, and left. I had a lot of things on my mind. I had to complete another volume of my collected oeuvres. I also hoped to enrich my vocabulary, and there's no better place for that than Africa. Furthermore, having just completed an article about Africa's shrinking land mass, I now could determine if my article was correct. And then, it occurred to me that I might also run into Alva.

Africa is a training ground for our technocrats. They come here for their initial training, hoping to complete it before Africa disappears. The doctors, the pharmacists, the engineers, the scientists, all studying their professions, so that one day they'll know how not to make mistakes. But there's not much time left.

Vanishing Africa, vanishing Alva, vanishing African armies

swallowed up in the bush, in the jungles, vanishing alligators, apes and ants. Africa is a favorite topic in literature, it gives license to so much excess, and now to a shrinking land mass. Lake Victoria is being drained to stop the Ugandans from crossing by boat.

I am visibly moved by the spirit, the patience, the unflagging energy of the moving crew from Upper Volta, as they, at least half a million men, quickly and expertly move and transplant trees and low hills, and entire settlements, from the eastern and western edges, since the edges are the first to vanish. Each day the coastline of Africa is changing. Undoubtedly this has affected the torpor-ridden population, has affected their melancholic outlook. Queen Quat after months of indecision has finally permitted one of her foreign advisers to indicate on the palace maps the extent of the land shrinkage. Admittedly it now takes fewer painters to cover the entire surface of Tanzania. Africa is diminishing in size. It is considerably smaller than all the pocket atlases indicate. Still, it is roomy enough for an Abercrombie & Fitch organized outing, six or seven men in bush jackets accompanied by fifty black gun carriers, basket carriers, tent carriers, but not more than fifty, since the now smaller Africa couldn't absorb it. Is it possible that I see Alva in their midst? All sitting down for a "Déjeuner sur l'herbe." How moving to think of Abercrombie & Fitch, full of devotion, ideals, valorously undertaking to dispatch another safari into this incredibly varied and vanishing land mass. Still the vocabulary remains the same. And Abercrombie's pocket dictionary is still useful. In time the dictionary may become the only record of Africa's obsolesence.

The Queen, seeing me off, jovially said in her slightly high-pitched voice: Next month I intend to produce a much more durable orange paint. She is seeing me off. She may never see me again, and she's still on the subject of paint.

58

WHY WRITE, the bushmen in Walikale asked me. Why write if you can use semaphore or smoke signals? I wouldn't want it any other way, I said. I came here in order to rehearse what I will say when I meet Alva in a Dar es Salaam bookstore.

We leave the tent at night, and briefly, there in the dark, in the thick forest, consider the silence that sustains Africa in our minds. Afterward, back inside the tent, reclining on our cots, we relax. Later, much later that night I think I can hear the sea, but we're hundreds of miles from the coast.

The three of us use few words, but we use them correctly, precisely, we use them without any hesitation, any lingering doubt or fear. We are all dressed alike, and we all have the same equipment. Unlike me, they are professionals, but we do not explore our differences. We are all white, and although our skins are not the same shade of white, had we been here a hundred years ago, we would most likely have been trading in guns or slaves.

Tomorrow we intend to have a crack at climbing Kilimanjaro, just for the pleasure of it. Both Bob and Boyd are discreet. They do not question me about Antibes, about my relationship with Nicholas's wife, or refer to the missing gold ornaments. They read the newspaper clippings, but they do not attempt to go through my papers. I assume they know I am a writer, but I may be mistaken about that.

At night, in front of a fire, we sit and exchange a few words. Both of the men are expert gunmen. They wouldn't think twice about killing someone for a few thousand dollars. Two thousand precisely. We get along well. I show them the newspaper clippings containing the photographs of Alex and Allen, although their appearance may have changed somewhat after all this time in the bush. I doubt if anyone will miss the two. The next morning, when I wake up, Bob and Boyd are outside doing some target practice. It never occurred to me to be afraid. Not for one moment.

XENOPHON SHOWED a misplaced courage. Instead of founding a new city, or settling down, or simply heading for Africa, he and his cast of ten thousand headed back home, as if there existed no other alternative. Xenophon's hold on history is clearly slipping. His tomb is cracking.

YOU WERE UNAWARE of me at first. You look up, surprised, not having heard what I said. You remind me of someone I knew in Antibes years ago. The book you are holding in your hand happens to be one I wrote. Yes, I happen to be the author. I was passing by and saw you holding it. I couldn't resist. You look at me, and then down at the book, as if searching for some confirmation. I entered the bookstore on an impulse, a combination of certain favorable signs. I was curious to know what you thought of the book, but obviously you hadn't read it. You were browsing. I am leaving Africa in a few hours, I explained. I had some business to attend to. I hope you enjoyed your stay, you said.

Outside this bookstore Africans are going about their business, transplanting Africa before it vanishes. The edges are crumbling away, slowly, gradually, but there's no panic. People go about their business, inventing new ways of carrying boxes on their heads, and building giant dams, and working on a new handwriting. Although, according to Lévi-Strauss, handwriting in Africa has been used in the past principally to exploit its people. You seemed a bit uncertain about this. But you agreed when I said that it was high time to return to the source. In a way, my old bush jacket is my source. It has four bulky pockets containing the gold ornaments. The jacket fed my imagination long before I ever set foot on this continent.

An hour later, sitting in an outdoor café, you smiled when I said that everything around us seemed so perfect. If I were to invent Africa all over again, I would not change a thing. I'd introduce a few broad tree-lined avenues, an outdoor café, a puppet theater and a realistic cannon pointing at the airport from which I will be leaving in another two hours.

You smiled.

You know, I said. You remind me so much of someone I know.

Z

ZAMBIA HELPS FILL OUR ZOOS, and our doubts, and our extrawide screens as we sit back. Each year we zigzag between the cages, prodding the alligators, the antelopes, the giant ants, just to see them move about a bit, just to make our life more authentic, to help us recapture the fantasy we had while watching the wide-screen spectacular with Rock Hudson on horseback, or the African Queen zapping Panda, the wild leopard. I stayed in Africa for a few weeks. Took the tours. Met a few people. Met Quat again. He's a great fellow. I had my photograph taken together with him. As a memento he gave me a few trinkets. Use them well, he said. After a short stay in East Africa, where I climbed Kilimanjaro, I flew to Dar es Salaam. It is surprising, really, that after traveling all over Africa, and confirming my suspicions regarding Africa's shrinking land mass, only one single incident keeps recurring in my mind.

Z

ZANZIBAR IS CLEARLY MARKED on the map. It is an unforgettable island with picturesque clusters of whitewashed houses surfacing here and there among the giant mangrove trees. The battered-looking fortification built by Arab slave traders on a hilltop overlooking the main port of the city of Zanzibar is also marked on the map. It is one of the few conspicuous landmarks that still remain. At sunset the view from up there can be breathtaking. In the hot summer evenings the whites used to drive up the narrow winding road in horse-drawn carriages, to relax on the ramparts of the fortification, where they would sip gin and tonic as they stared across at the mainland. Everyone is acutely aware that Zanzibar is an island. It is within shouting distance of Africa. Shouting across to the mainland is a popular pastime over here. Each evening men who have spent the day cutting sugar cane get together on the main pier and boisterously shout Swahili obscenities across to the mainland. That's how a culture takes shape, observed the French Consul pointedly. That's how a language acquires a new resonance, a preciseness and depth. Alfred did not say anything at all. Everything the Consul said or did made him feel profoundly uncomfortable. Clearly, he felt it was to his advantage to say as little as possible. Only Alva, completely unafraid as ever, responded. Zanzibar, I believe, is a part of

Africa, she said. Yes, said the Consul. There was every reason to believe it was, because of the island's extreme proximity to the African mainland. Alva nodded. She'd never really given Zanzibar more than just a passing thought. But it was reassuring, she said, to encounter a form of life on this island that is so familiar.

Just to see the women having their hair done in the beauty parlors has made me feel at home.

Have you noticed, remarked the French Consul, that most of the local women are wearing wrist watches. You see, I do believe that in principle they have accepted the conditions, or if you will, the tyranny of time passing . . . and now, like the whites and the Arab traders, they pretend that time exists. Why, in order to impress this illusion upon each other, continues the French Consul enthusiastically, evidently carried away by the daring of his hypothesis, the women visit the beauty parlors simply in order to have a reason to consult their watches.

Alfred slowly nods his head affirmatively. His vacuous face conceals an instant distrust of the Consul's attempt to charm Alva.

Alva doesn't wear a watch. She can undress in less than three minutes, but everything she does in bed is timeless.

Unfortunately you've come at the wrong time, said the French Consul by way of a greeting when they arrived. Everyone is getting out. Everyone is packing and preparing to leave the island. A familiar scene somehow. The wealthy are the first to leave, departing in their cars and in rented trucks which are ferried across to the mainland. Alfred is only nineteen. He doesn't ask many questions. He would if he knew what to ask. Alva, however, is never at a loss for a question, promptly inquiring where she can buy some cheap ivory trinkets. She and

Alfred together don't have more than a few words of Swahili, and most of the words are not very useful. She knows that

Zaa implies the vital male and female reproduction, and Zaba means to hit or beat, and

Zabadi is the substance taken from a civet cat and used in perfume, and

Zafe, a noun, means slime and slipperiness, and

Zahama, also Zahimu, means confusion, noise, oppression and distress, and

Zaini, is to cheat, deceive or persuade to do wrong, and

Zengea is to search for, and Zimvi is a spirit, a demon or a fairy.

Tell me, says the French Consul as soon as he and Alfred are alone. Is she passionate? Alfred hesitated. She looks it says the Consul cheerfully, much to Alfred's relief obviating a reply to the unexpected question.

On their third day Alfred impetuously buys a twenty-seven room villa for twenty dollars and three cartons of Philip Morris cigarettes. So now they have three bathrooms with hot and cold running water, two kitchens, a large garden with fifteen fruit trees, but everything is a bit run down and neglected. Most of the windows have been smashed by vandals, and there are bullet holes in the walls. But for twenty dollars it seemed an outright bargain. Alfred bought the building without even inspecting it. He doesn't even know if he bought it from its owner. Don't you think that you should have at least asked the man for some kind of a receipt and a bill of sale to prove your ownership, says Alva. She also would have liked some more information about the family that had lived in the house before. Some of their clothes are still hanging in the bedroom closet, and their photographs are on a marble mantelpiece imported from Italy. It's really most unusual, says Alva.

Zanzibar is still on the map. The atlas she and Alfred are using is the one Allen acquired secondhand years ago in Antibes. It was printed just after the Second World War. It contains some interesting facts about Zanzibar, says Alfred. But these facts, from a quick glance at the surrounding countryside, no longer seem of overriding importance.

Alva cut out Zanzibar with a pair of scissors and placed it on the table. She wanted Alfred to face the issue. It's just the kind of thing a woman would do under the circumstances. Confront the true issues. Alfred rather enjoyed being the owner of a house, and pretended not to notice. Angrily Alva next turned to Zaire. Only on the map she is cutting up, Zaire is still called the Belgian Congo. There are some interesting facts as well in the atlas about the Belgian Congo. She calmly continues cutting out the Congo, now called Zaire, while Alfred nervously bites his nails. Although he is in his heart of hearts reconciled to the eventual loss of Zanzibar, and his holdings which amount to a twenty dollar investment, he is not yet prepared to discard Zaire. For one thing, it is so much larger. There are so many more people, and so many more possibilities for someone his age. At night when Alfred, who is only nineteen, tries to embrace Alva, she turns her back to him. He is again being rejected. A familiar situation. Alfred was an only child. He grew up in a large house, and only at the age of three learned with great difficulty to distinguish the interior from the exterior. Zanzibar's dogs learn to do the same at a much earlier age. They catch on much faster. Yet all their activities to some extent seem to depend on human whim. Trying to fall asleep, Alfred thinks how much worse the dogs have it.

During the recent riots a good many doors and gates had

been smashed, giving the dogs greater freedom of movement. All the same, quite a few end up in a pot, said the Consul, warning him not to eat meat in the local restaurants. Having with his own eyes seen a couple of mangy and emaciated dogs in the street, Alfred tries not to think of yesterday's dinner. If he ate a dog he sincerely regrets it now. He tries not to think of it. Instead he thinks of Alva. To be only nineteen and to have made love to her. In his notebook he had marked the number of times. Sixteen, no seventeen, actually eighteen if he counted the one time outdoors.

Zanzibar is only a short distance from the African mainland. Alva can tell the distance from looking at her somewhat mutilated atlas, and from looking out of her bedroom window. Everything she does, no matter how trivial it is, somehow reminds her of her past, and of all the men in her life who professed to adore her slender back, her breasts, her long white legs. Each time she walks over to the window to confirm Africa's proximity, or simply to see how the sun is doing, she seems to be reviving a past love affair. Naked she walks to the window. She is repeating something she has done over a thousand times. One never knows when one does anything for the last time. All over Zanzibar tall and lithe black men with smooth glistening faces are overtly rubbing their crotches whenever they see Alva passing. She can't wait for Alfred, little Alfred to come down with food poisoning. She'll slip out for a few hours. Is it any wonder that Alfred is amazed at her unpredictability. Where have you been this afternoon, Alfred asks her. I have been staring out of the window, she replies.

It must be the zucchini, Alva tells Alfred whose face has turned a deathly chalk white.

I'll never touch the stuff again, he says.

It must be the zucchini.

Promise me, he says, that you'll never mention the word again.

What word, she asks innocently.

The French Consul and his wife have invited Alva to dinner at the consulate. The formal engraved invitation was delivered by a black servant. It excluded Alfred. Alva spent the entire day preparing for the dinner. At five she told Alfred that she was going out for a walk. Seeing that she was all dressed up, he said nothing. Bitterness sealed his lips. At least four hundred men sensuously rubbed their crotches as Alva passed them on the street. Somewhere a dog howled piercingly. To her astonishment Alva is the only guest for dinner. The French Consul introduces her to his radiant-faced wife. Having spent the last twenty years in Zanzibar, the French Consul is exceedingly well informed. He seems almost eager to impart some of his vast knowledge to Alva. In 1942, he informs her, there were two hundred policemen in Zanzibar, give or take a dozen. That would be approximately one policeman to every 1,324.36 inhabitants, using the 1948 population census, or one policeman to every 1,210 inhabitants, using the 1938 population estimate. In 1942 the two hundred policemen remained quite unconcerned by the fate of France or England. Many of them would come to me with their problems. They were fine men, said the Consul wistfully. They all had a few words of French, although Tanzania was still an English protectorate. But they preferred French. I used to fill the gap with Swahili, using words like Zuia, which means, to stop, to keep back or restrain; and Zuri, which means to commit perjury or swear falsely. At that time those were absolutely essential words for one's day-to-day encounters. Of course, by now most of the two hundred men have either retired or had their throats cut. . . While the Consul is explaining why most of the bourgeoisie had abandoned or sold their homes in some cases for less than twenty dollars, Alva feels a leg stealthily rubbing against her leg underneath the table. Although surreptitious, it is an exceedingly practiced kind of pressure, Alva decides. Almost everyone who has remained in Zanzibar, continues the Consul, is now contentedly living in a villa, eating dogs and zucchini. Alva looked searchingly at the Consul and at his radiant-faced wife who is at least twenty years younger than her husband, without being able to determine whose leg was pressing against her leg.

The French Consul continues to regale his visitor with the eventful history of the island, a history that has yet to be written in French or English. Admittedly there were some Africans who considered themselves historians, although in his opinion they were simply former guides who had escorted the tourists around the island. In 1948 there were approximately one to every 88,624 inhabitants, which compares favorably to the ratio of historians in France and the United States. The historians had stopped working as guides out of pique . . . they wished to write history, not simply chat about it.

When the Consul got up from the table, the pressure on Alva's leg did not decrease, as she had anticipated. On the contrary, it increased, it became, if anything, more brazen, more overt, as if her acquiescence had all along been taken for granted. Alva glanced at the serene and beautiful face of the Consul's young wife, and overcoming any scruples she may have had, quickly adjusted herself to the unexpected situation.

Still, reflected the Consul, puffing away at a cigar, I think we are managing quite well without the participation of the native historians. They'd only confuse everything. For instance they kept lumping all the different tribes that exist on the mainland under one name, Umyamwezi. Umyamwezi is a Kinyamwezi word, and means, country of Mwezi. Mwezi is a country of ill-defined limits which supposedly lies between the parallels 2 degrees to 7 degrees latitude and 31 degrees to 34 degrees longitude, and having an area of about 55,000 square miles. Needless to say, the Consul declared rather vigorously, there is no such country. Still, in 1948 these quasi-historians were frequently consulted by the soon to be independent African nations, who were straining at their leash, ready to advance, ready to annihilate the ant kingdom at a word, a single word. I suppose this went to their heads. When they quit their jobs as tourist guides, the entire police force became demoralized. They threatened to mutiny, but their mutiny was quickly put down. For lack of something better to do, the Consul explained, he had walked into a deserted police station a week ago, and gone through their reports to see if there was any mention of the native historians. But it was all routine. Accusations, blackmail, torture, a few severed heads and some dog eating records as far back as 1934, but no mention of the historians.

At eleven the Consul retired for the night. Alva and the Consul's wife embraced. They kissed feverishly, hungrily . . . as they tore off their clothes, compressing the excitement of their experience into their moans, which might have led someone in the distance to believe that they were speaking Swahili. The day before Alfred had written home: finally I am no longer alone. But everything that was taking place was falling short of his expectations.

Zanzibar is still within shouting distance of the mainland, but there doesn't seem to be anyone to whom one can shout across. The people on the other side seem to speak a different language, and as everyone knows, languages form attitudes.

Still, there is some desultory trading. It is carried on in the accepted Zanzibar fashion. None of the ancient mistrust has ever been eradicated. The men from Zanzibar row across to the mainland, and arrange their goods, most of which they have stolen from empty and abandoned villas and warehouses, in neat rows along the beach. Then rowing back to what they consider a safe distance they shrilly whistle until the mainlanders arrive. The mainlanders, in turn, flock to the beach, eagerly examining the goods, trying on the clothes to see if they fit. Then without removing one article, they place a few bags of gold dust on the sand near the goods, and signaling to the men in the boat, they leave. The men from Zanzibar row back to the shore and pick up the gold. If they're not satisfied with the amount, they row back to a safe distance, having left everything as they found it. The mainlanders return to the beach as soon as they hear the signal. Either they add another bag of gold dust, or they remove their gold altogether. It is a long drawn-out affair, and requires nerves of steel. The French Consul once accompanied a trading party, and was able to witness history, as he called it, unfold right in front of his eyes.

Alfred is still feeling wretched. Alva is away most of the time. She is visiting the wife of the French Consul. Both spend the entire day in bed, oblivious of the black men crouching outside the wrought-iron gate of the French consulate, oblivious of everything but the beauty of their private pleasure.

Y

YOU MUST AVOID having nothing to say and nothing to do in this heat, the French Consul said to Alfred. It can cause irreparable damage to your nervous system. I would strongly advise you to make effective use of all the Swahili words in your limited vocabulary, if you wish to survive. Still not fully recovered from his recent illness, his two weeks in bed, Alfred, still looking sickly, looked uneasily at the Consul, mumbling, yes, not out of a conviction, but from a desire to stem the latter's flow of words, to appease this intellectual tyrant, this jabbering magpie.

Yes . . . well, now where were we? asked the Consul. He is the only diplomat left on the island. But if he has survived it is not because of his dapper appearance, his immaculate appearance, or because of his uniform and medals, or because of his slightly effeminate gestures, or because of his white hair.

I was terribly upset when, upon my arrival, I first saw all those men gleefully rubbing their genitals outside the consulate, said the Consul's wife. Alva admired her poise, her frozen beauty and her large wardrobe. Help yourself to anything that catches your eye, said the Consul's wife sweetly. Then, after Alva had gratefully kissed the Consul's wife, they spoke some more Swahili.

Alfred may have been only nineteen, but he already knew

74

that every object at the consulate had a purpose. He could tell at a glance that a considerable amount of attention had been paid to the placement of each piece of furniture. Nothing appeared random or haphazard except, possibly, his own presence.

I'm sorry that you had to walk, said the Consul, but all the buses and taxis have stopped running because of the acute shortage of gasoline and spare parts, not to mention the shortage of passengers. The Consul laughed a wheezing choking laugh that left a dry rattling sound in his throat after the laugh had subsided. Alfred is only nineteen. But at nineteen Rimbaud, having escaped from Verlaine's prick, came here to make his fortune. This alone, and the knowledge that he is the owner of a twenty-seven room villa, keeps Alfred from drowning in despair.

I never get tired of listening to the sounds of Africa, said the Consul, motioning with his hand in the direction of the window. Alfred assumed that the Consul was referring to the incessant drum beats which had been keeping him awake at night. The distant sound of the drums seemed to emanate from the northern section of the island, from the thick and impenetrable forest. The sound infuriated Alfred, it also dislocated his sense of direction. It had taken him the better part of an hour to find the consulate. When he finally caught sight of the wrought-iron gate of the consulate, he broke into a run.

The drums are announcing Alva's presence, the shape of her footprints, the texture of her skin and descriptions of her long white legs, her breasts, her ankles, her neck, the color of her faded dress, of her eyes, of her long hair and of the ornaments, the silver ornaments she is wearing on her wrists. The drums also list the names of the servants who are still working at the consulate, the only consulate still flying a foreign flag. The drum beats are audible throughout the night. Perhaps if he listened long enough, thought Alfred, he might even get to hear a description of Verlaine's prick, a thin puny affair.

How is it that unlike all the others you've managed to stay on the island, Alva asked the French Consul.

My dear, I am so glad that chance brought you here. I haven't seen my wife look so happy in years. Finally she has someone to speak to.

You haven't answered my question, she says playfully.

Despite appearances to the contrary, the French Consul's life has also been disrupted. He keeps sending lengthy detailed reports and letters marked confidential to the French Foreign Office, urging them to recognize his predicament at having to deal with people in government who no longer speak a fluent French. But he is stretching the truth somewhat when he refers to a government, since none seems to exist on the island.

Day and night the drums keep up their heavy incessant beat, a beat that is occasionally interspersed by a few minutes of silence. The drum's message penetrates the thick white-washed walls of the consulate. In effect, the drums describe the artful and civilized interior of the consulate, as it has been described by the servants working at the consulate. Each day one of the servants will walk to the forest and in minute detail describe what has taken place at the consulate on the previous day, and what might have happened, as well as what didn't happen . . . naturally, for the sake of brevity, the drums abbreviate a lot. Is it possible that the description of Verlaine's prick could have been made by the Consul?

The Consul rose at seven-thirty. His wife, as usual, sleeping in a separate room, slept late. Unlike him, she had her breakfast, croissant, mushroom omelette and coffee, in bed. The visitor, sleeping in an adjacent room, slept late as well. The visitor joined the Consul's wife in bed. They both shared her breakfast. They both spoke excitedly about all the things they missed living here. Unlike Rimbaud, the Consul's wife doesn't contemplate escaping her husband's prick, although certain parallels between the Consul and Verlaine could be drawn.

On the southern tip of the island a small army of men is furtively training with automatic rifles, bazookas, two-inch mortars and hand grenades. But they are not very experienced, some of the soldiers being only nine years old. They intend to attack the great warrior ants, the ferocious driver ants, sometime in the near future. They intend to rid the island of its ants. It will be a savage battle, at times a one-sided battle as Africans will churn up dust, crush grass, as they advance against the colonies of ants . . .

The French Consul has all kinds of ailments, yet he doesn't despair. He also has a large bathroom with blue tiles which he doesn't share with his wife. He has a large library which he doesn't share with her either. He also has a handsome mahogany desk, circa 1760, with nine drawers on either side, upon which he writes his reports and his letters. Most of the letters begin with: Your Excellency, or Dear General, or My Dear Count, or Dear Baroness, or My Dear Brother, or Most Illustrious and Reverend Lord, or Charlie, or Dear Poppsie, but never Dear Sir. He is an excellent speller, and hardly ever consults a dictionary, unless he is writing in German. Since he never locks any of the nine drawers on either side of his desk, it is no surprise that the drums are able to pinpoint his thoughts, his preoccupations, his excremental vision, his precise location in his house. His habits may not be African habits . . . but they are absorbing, they are intriguing, they help pass the time for everyone. Listening to the drums, all the people on the island feel a little less lonely.

77

The drums also pay tribute to the exceptionally fine Queen Anne period bookcase in burr walnut of superb faded colors, the silver-case skull watch, the Hepplewhite wheelback chairs and the French Consul in his dinner jacket, tirelessly recording in his notebook all the changes, the ominous cracks in the ceiling, the peeling wallpaper, the worn patches in the rugs and the scuttling sound of unseen rats, as the servants become more and more rebellious, retreating into a kind of sullen silence, although he, the French Consul, tries to pacify their anger by speaking about Marx, and how a freshly recruited army of nine year olds would cross over and attack the mainland, creating the United Republic of Tanzania, and, in any event, how they, the servants, were free to drive up to the former fortification at any time on their day off, and drink a cold glass of beer while taking in the breathtaking view of the mainland.

You must find something to do, the French Consul tells Alfred. You can't stay in the twenty-seven room house by yourself. You'll soon retreat into yourself, become a recluse, abandon language and thought. You'll lose more and more words. We mustn't let that happen to you.

What should I do, Alfred asked helplessly.

So the Consul hires him on the spot to take an inventory of the entire island. He thought up the job on the spur of the moment, feeling a certain obligation, a certain duty toward Alfred, after all he was partly to blame for Alfred's unhappiness.

Try to be as accurate as possible, said the Consul. In some instances a rough estimate will have to do. You may find some of the reports in the deserted police stations quite useful.

What should I include in the inventory, asks Alfred.

Everything! . . .

Alfred is carried away by an excitement he cannot quite articulate. His face has turned a deep shade of red. He blinks his eyes rapidly. He feels he is on the threshold of success, and in his mind there flashes the spectacle of himself as Rimbaud, outwitting Verlaine, outwitting Africa, outwitting France. Still, he is not certain what the French Consul really wants. An inventory? Surreptitiously he wipes his perspiring palms on his trouser legs.

You may need some assistance, said the Consul. I'll have a hundred men waiting for you on Monday. I suggest you divide them into teams of four men each. Be very explicit when you ask them for anything, and for heaven's sake, stay away from politics. They are so easily frustrated. You speak some Swahili, don't you? Alfred lies. A few words, he says.

Good, it'll come in useful.

Where exactly would you like me to start, asked Alfred timidly.

We'll have to play that by ear, said the Consul, tugging at one ear lobe.

Alfred has been reading Rimbaud and dropping acid. He is nervous. His legs and hands tingle from nervousness. Alva's prolonged absence has done nothing to relieve his nervousness. The lush tropical foliage does not soothe him. Despondently he examines Alva's clothes, the contents of her handbag. He comes across the names of Alex, Allen and Quat, but the names don't mean anything to him. He is high on acid and nervously paces up and down the length of the room. Finally he steps out of the window, since it appears to be the quickest way to see Africa. Fortunately he lands unhurt in the thick elephant grass one story below. He has fallen on top of a group of people picnicking in the grass. He picks himself up and apologizes. When they fail to respond, he has a closer look at their waxen faces. They resemble the people in the photographs that are so neatly arranged on the marble mantelpiece inside the house.

How curious, he says to himself. He would have gone inside to have another look at the photographs, but couldn't locate the entrance. Instead he went for a walk. He is the only white in sight. But no one pays the slightest attention to him. He poked his head into a few small stores. Even in his present state he found them unprepossessing. He tried to think of something to buy. But his needs, for the moment, were so to speak, taken care of.

Five hours earlier he had triumphantly emerged from the French consulate carrying a Swahili-English dictionary. Entering a store, he thought he would exchange a few words with these people. The first word he said was, Yakini: which means truth. And Wataka Yakini gani? which means: what sort of proof do you want? And Yumba, which means, to sway like a drunken person, and Yungyung, which means, a worm, and Nayakini kukoja jana kwangu, which means, I am sure you did not come to my house yesterday.

He is engulfed by African riotous laughter, loud shrill laughter. After all he has been seen passing through the massive wrought-iron gates of the Consulate, and the wrought-iron design of the gates is deeply embedded in the African mind.

X

X STANDS FOR EXPERIMENTAL, and for excretion, that is for plain shit on the trail. Avoid the trails marked with an X. Avoid the driver ants. But X is just another notation, another abbreviation, another warning. Look for the X before you take another step. There are no words that begin with the letter X in the Swahili-English dictionary. X is a European precaution, explained the French Consul. He always made himself available when Alfred came to visit. He would drop *Anabasis*, or whatever else he happened to be reading, and willingly address himself to Alfred's baffled silence. For Alfred, silence was a precaution, although he kept battling against his silence. He attempted to thrust words into that total void. Mostly the words he used were monosyllabic, such as, huh and no.

Last May the entire Muslim population fled the island, said the Consul. There must have been at least ten thousand of them. But lacking a leader, someone like Xenophon to lead their march, to record their history, their bravery, or perhaps simply to stimulate it . . . at any rate, lacking a Xenophon who admired the Spartans, and who later capitalized on his experiences, withdrawing to the country to write about his experiences, they, the ten thousand Muslims, took a wrong turn upon reaching the mainland, losing their way in the jungles where most of them were killed by driver ants.

Alfred wanted to ask when he would get paid for the inventory, but he couldn't find the right phrase. The correct phrase.

The Africa I know is getting smaller, said the Consul morosely. It is also, quite inexplicably, turning orange. I have been studying the mainland through my telescope. I don't know what to make of it.

For Alfred, these visits to the consulate had acquired an enormous significance. Finally he was involved in a dialogue. It was a dialogue that belonged only to him and the French Consul. Dialogues can flare up, he discovered, without warning, without any premeditation, although the surroundings, the seventeenth-century armchair, the oak buffet, the inlaid floor tiles, the wrought-iron candlestick, the gold-embroidered cushion, did much to enhance whatever the Consul was saying. The words he uttered were in the strictest sense directed at Alfred, and in that respect, Alfred was free to take them with him, and do with them whatever he wanted. They were words, and they conveyed a certain meaning as well as a distinct flavor, a somewhat dry brittle intelligence at work, an intelligence that was beginning to crumble and disintegrate in the tropics, like the handsome furniture that had been brought over from France. At any rate, just as dialogues can flare up, they can with unexpected suddeness be extinguished. The slightest interruption can be fatal. It can lead one or the other participant in the conversation to evaluate the situation, and perhaps find it wanting. He is not speaking to me, decides Alfred. He is speaking to himself. My presence enables him to speak to himself.

This time the French Consul did nothing to prevent him from seeing Alva. She was wearing one of Jacqueline's dresses. To Alfred's surprise, she said: I'm so happy to hear about the inventory. Clearly, it seemed to him, that she had him at a disadvantage. Somehow the arrangement of the furniture, if nothing else, inhibited him from expressing his feelings. Later in the day he smashed a couple of windows in his house, shouting: those fucking shitheads . . . do they take me for Verlaine's prick.

WHEN ALEX AND ALLEN arrived in Tanzania they had almost run out of cash. A day after their arrival they lost their faithful African guide to a man-eating snake. But they also managed to pick up a few words of Swahili. Just enough to get by.

Wahiji means appearance in Swahili. Therefore, when they arrived at a small town they asked the first man they met: Unamjua Quat? Utaweza kuniambia wajihi wake. To which the man replied that he didn't know Quat, and not knowing Quat, he couldn't say what he looked like.

They had been traveling for months. One month blending into the next. The distinctions between the different tropical plants, and between the different wild animals becoming, somehow, less and less noticeable. By the time they reached Tanzania they felt as if they had been circling one large tree, followed at a safe distance, by one bird, a vulture. We have reached the oneness of all things, declared Alex philosophically. We have reached the end of our tether. We have reached the ultimate.

When Queen Quat offered them a plateful of biscuits, they each unashamedly took a handful. So much for the one-ness. They had just had a filling Tanzanian meal, but their recent deprivation had left its mark on them.

When Alex mentioned the past, that is to say, when he mentioned Antibes, the dead jeweler, the small apartment overlooking the Mediterranean, the bar, the occasional trip to Nice, the Queen diffidently listened, and then promptly changed the subject. In Africa, just as anywhere else, when a new subject is introduced the old one is discarded, is obliterated, is erased from the memory as if it had never been mentioned in the first place. To bring it up again requires persistance, requires courage and stamina. It is at this moment that Alex and Allen discovered the extent of their helplessness.

Later, when Alex furiously attacked Allen for not supporting him, for not forcing Quat to respond to his remarks, Allen got out of bed, put on a robe and left the room.

After several hours Alex began to have grave misgivings about Allen's absence. He began to have grave doubts and suspicions. Not even his total and utter dejectedness could prevent him from indulging in a self-defeating contemplation of his existence. Most likely he would have searched the palace had he not found the door to his room locked, and a guard outside his window.

The next morning at breakfast Alex brazenly mentioned the missing gold trinkets. The Queen suggested that they had never existed. After all, she reasoned, the three of them had intended to kidnap the jeweler and hold him for a ransom. As far as she could recollect, there had been no mention of any jewelry.

Right, said Allen.

Clearly he was not to be trusted any longer, decided Alex.

Perhaps Alex had been in a hypnotic trance, said the Queen. Perhaps he had imagined a briefcase.

Allen smiled derisively. Later he confided to Alex that the Queen had asked him to stay.

Well, what's keeping Allen, jeered Alex.

Allen never referred to the Queen's invitation again, but

after what she had told him, he looked at Alex with less respect. Leave that prick, the Queen had said. He's a loser.

On Monday morning Alfred was informed by a messenger from the consulate that some men who were to assist him with the inventory were waiting for him in the main square.

How many men, he asked.

Several hundred, replied the messenger.

I'll not be intimidated by Verlaine's shriveled white prick, Alfred thought. Although Verlaine's prick did not seem relevant at that moment, the thought gave him courage. Nevertheless, when he caught sight of the assembled men, his legs trembled, and he kept clearing his throat nervously, although he hadn't opened his mouth to speak. The drum beats were still audible, but now they were soft as if cushioned with rose petals. Can they, he wondered, discern the disorder of my mind.

Together, he heard himself saying, we shall count the people, the animals, the trees, the houses, one story, two story, brick, mud, frame, the huts, the roads, paved or dirt roads, the cars, the telephones, the outhouses . . . I have a list in my hand . . .

This will take considerably longer than I anticipated, Alfred told the French Consul that afternoon.

Excellent, said the Consul. I like the way it is being handled. I'm so glad I thought of it.

To begin with, I think we need a new population census.

Right. Remind me later. I'll have everyone assemble in the square tomorrow morning. It should be a simple matter to count the . . .

On second thought, interjected Alfred hastily, perhaps we better postpone it.

Everything that is not hidden is visible. Alva has no reason to hide her breasts. In the bedroom, she and Jacqueline are locked in a deep embrace. They are grunting and growling. The servants are perfectly aware of what is going on inside their room, but like most servants they respect the privacy of the bedroom. The following day one of them went to the forest and reported: Washenzi walikuwa uchi, which meant, the savages were naked.

I'm leaving my husband and returning to Paris, said Jacqueline. Do join me.

Alva impulsively said, OK. But neither meant it. Neither was sincere in her love. Sex was engrossing because, and only because, neither was infected by the French Consul's passion for history.

The servant, who had gone to the forest to report what had happened in the bedroom, did not return.

Another one, sighed the French Consul. Mysteries played havoc with his imagination. He was quite prepared to anticipate another uprising, and therefore clung to every inexplicable event . . .

Alfred thinks: nothing is the same.

V

VANISHING IN AFRICA, thought Shirley as she read the post card I had sent her. The architectural rendering of Queen Quat's palace on the post card had been printed in Switzerland. I chose it because of the two vanishing points to the left and right of the palace. Vanishing points are simply an architectural contrivance, but to me they are also an appropriate explanation for my conduct.

He's vacationing in Africa, thought Shirley. After her husband's untimely death, she inherited the house, the jewelry business, the gleaming furniture, the dog. The children are at school when the mailman arrives to deliver the mail. The gray-haired terrier is growling at the door. Shirley's memories resemble the diamond rings in her dead husband's store. Each memory is embedded in a separate velvet-lined box. I see no reason to stay alone by myself, Shirley explains to her mother, to the children, to the grocer, the butcher and the mailman, but they continue to stare at her accusingly.

How long has he been gone? one of the men she recently met in a bar asked her.

She doesn't recall. Her mind is on something else. Presently she is thinking about a tear in her madras skirt. The skirt lies neatly folded on a chair next to her blouse. The two men are staying in a familiar-looking hotel room. The colorful outside is concealed by several layers of paint, plaster, brick, concrete and a fireproof curtain. The interior does not resemble an African palace. It is too functional. The meaning of each object, like that of her presence, can be easily discerned.

The card from Africa is in her purse, so are her keys, and a photograph of her children, and her late husband, and some cash, and make up, but no calendar, no charts, no record of my visits. It is pointless to search the handbag.

I haven't been inside a hotel room for ages, said Shirley, sitting on a couch, making herself very small. The explicit purpose of the hotel furniture appears to overwhelm them. So far she actually finds something attractive in being afraid. Her presence in their room has become an obstacle to their freedom. As she removes her shoes, her skirt, her blouse, the obstacles increase. The two men concentrate on the buoyant carefree life outside that now seems almost unattainable. Fate glides on oiled hinges toward the bathroom, then to the bed, then again to the bathroom . . . People outside nervously observe the traffic signals, but otherwise nothing impedes their gratuitous and even murderous disdain of the grid pattern of the streets. They slip in and out of houses. Open and close doors, never once looking at the doorknobs or the sky. Now her legs are spread apart as both men stare a bit fearfully at the vanishing point. The irresolvable architectonic point of departure.

Does it blow the mind, she asks.

No further details are necessary. The orange carpet, the olive-green plastic shower curtain at this moment serve no useful purpose. Still they are there, awaiting a future use.

Shirley is the only female in the room. This is made evident by their behavior. Everyone relies to some extent on past behavior. Shirley's female past is securely sheltered in a jewelry case. She invites both men to visit her sometime, preferably at a time when her children are at school or asleep. Everything she does remains in a female context. Before she leaves, both men admit that they are looking for me because I once insulted a female member of their family. They had not intended to tell her this, but they now sense her sympathy.

He also has insulted me, she says softly.

U

UPON MY ARRIVAL the gray-haired terrier barked frantically as I rang the doorbell. He came forward sniffing suspiciously at my shoes, at my trouser legs, sniffing the African earth, the African experience, the African landscape. I couldn't tell if he could discern the extent of my travels, of my underhand adventures, and if he could detect, from the suspicious bulges in the pockets of my bush jacket, their contents, those magnificently made African gold trinkets.

I have absolutely no friends at all, no feeling for this city, none since my car, my garage, my outdoor plants had been destroyed. Much to my amazement the Mediterranean sky, upon my return, had lost its luminous glow, and Antibes in the short space of time I had been away, had its old quarter, the most beautiful section in town, razed to the ground by real estate speculators. But the jewelry store is still standing. A few customers inside are bending over the glass showcases. An elderly man is inspecting some small carved pieces of ivory. Upon my return the dog barks. Quickly I feed it some scraps of meat I always keep in my pocket for just such an emergency. Shirley is remote and indifferent. She now has two lovers. She takes the express elevator to the eighteenth floor. She keeps her eyes focused on the middle distance, and remains impervious to the offensive language, the innuendoes, the banter, the guffaws of the men in the elevator. She can see through their intentions. By now she can see through doors. She comes here frequently, but lacking an outline, she remains undecided. Perhaps she'll separate the two good friends and marry one. But how to select one. She can hardly tell them apart. From the eighteenth floor one can take in the entire city, one can see the airport, and the harbor, and the two men stalking me.

A map of Africa can be drawn from memory by anyone having an elementary school education. I should add that the outlines of Africa can be drawn at one rapid sweep with a pen or pencil. One needn't even lift the pencil point from the paper unless one intends to include the turbulent island on the east coast. The island is another matter. Either it's the Arabs running the slave trade, or it's the uprising, or the island's driver ants. In any case, the mainlanders have always found the island's proximity more threatening and menacing than the island's dimension might suggest.

I have several new friends, Shirley said defiantly. To my satisfaction nothing has been changed in the house. Among Nicholas's books I locate a fascinating book entitled: *Die Ratsame und Nützliche Ausrottung der Gefährlichen Afrikanischen Ameisen.** My unexpected appearance has obviously disturbed Shirley, startled the children, and completely unnerved the terrier. None seemed prepared for my arrival. After all, I had already been replaced by two men, both being as near as I can tell the same height as Shirley's late husband, since his suits, shirts and shoes fit them to a T. This confuses the dog, and the children, not to mention the mailman, and the man coming to read the meter. Frequently, more frequently than I care to record, Shirley takes the elevator to the eighteenth floor. Habits form quickly. The men have long ago exhausted

* *The Advisable and Useful Extermination of the Dangerous African Ants.*

all questions regarding my trip to Africa, my intentions, my relationship to Alex and Allen, my books, my sexual quirks. They have never entirely lost their skepticism regarding the information Shirley so readily keeps feeding them. Most of the time they remain closeted in the hotel. They still accuse me of having insulted a female member of their immediate family. Both men are pale, since they stay away from the sun. The mere mention of my name brings an angry flush to their pale faces. The things I said to their sister, or is it niece, sit heavily on their rubber-soled brains. They massage their knuckles. They have never insulted a female in their life. Not they. They have only respect for female members. Intently they stare at Shirley. They have never once in her presence intentionally called her, or anyone else, a cunt, or a clit. But they do occasionally think of it. Their thoughts are frequently directed in that direction. It may explain the glazed look in their eyes as soon as she crosses her legs.

From outside, from the garden, a fragance of jasmine pervades the room. Having almost completed my complete oeuvres I am troubled by a surfeit of names, names like: Alex and Allen, Alva and Absalom, Afouganou and Bamileke, and Bwango and Dingaan, as they say or explain, respond or answer, murmur or retort, swallow or blush, fumble or tremble, gasping or clenching their teeth, as the doubt or certainty, hope or longing, dissolves, evaporates, is eradicated leaving an unsettling memory of a trip, a journey, a short hop to Africa, and a stay in a hut or tent among nervously laughing men with unpronounceable names, because my own nervousness is infectious. I am quite capable of infecting an entire continent, and have it share my misgivings, my doubts as I prepare to complete another book.

T

THEY ARE BOUND TO MEET. Sooner or later they are bound to run into each other. That much one can determine from the routes they have taken, and from their conversations, and from their maps, and from their mutual abhorrence of ants. But are they really going to run into each other. Merely being on a continent that is shrinking is not sufficient reason to meet. Particularly if the meeting might entail a disagreeable confrontation.

Perhaps Bob and Boyd might be less cruel if they had been raised in a more hospitable environment, and if they had had a more loving mother, and if they had discovered sexual gratification at an earlier age, and if they had not seen those African stag films. The two of them are always on the go. Everything they own is portable. Everything they own is lightweight or dispensable. Bob once fell in love. When Boyd discovered this, he promptly shot the girl, her parents and their animals, and set the farm on fire. Bob respected Boyd's feelings, and the dimension of his anger. The subject is never raised. Tactfully they avoid the topic. They also avoid girls, except for an occasional bash in the bush. Bob avoids falling in love again for fear that the past horrors might be repeated again.

As Bob and Boyd approach the east coast they meet men

who are transplanting Africa. The fact that the continent is actually shrinking has finally sunk in. Still, one can drive for hours through the bush and not see another soul. If things get really bad, they can always return home and serve a twenty-year to life sentence for murder. Like everyone else in Africa they depend on information. They listen to the drums. Reaching a large city they study all the posters in the post office. Basically they respond to information like everyone else. Their last client gave them four thousand dollars and a newspaper clipping from a French newspaper. For some inexplicable reason the client kept frequently changing his story. They had to assist him. They had to fill in the blanks each time he seemed at a loss for a name . . . Bob keeps the clipping in the pocket of his bush jacket. He has memorized the names of the two men they are supposed to locate. Their names are Alex and Allen. He has also committed their photographs to memory. Daily he refreshes his memory. But the newspaper clipping is turning a dark brown and that is affecting his memory. Still, four thousand can go far in Africa. Bob shows the clipping to everyone they meet. Both he and Boyd don't have any maps because the terrain is so familiar. They sleep like rocks at night. Their nostrils twitch at the slightest sound. All of Africa recognizes them. These cats have been around for ages, says Queen Quat. She always keeps a couple of hundred dollars in a plain envelope, just in case they drop in.

The changes caused by the shrinkage are confusing Boyd. Sometimes they clumsily bump into trees because they didn't expect any trees to be there. Still, their emotions have remained stable. They don't ponder over the past. They have no emotional response to their surroundings. They can be said to be functioning smoothly. Certain surroundings permit them to function more easily than others. They do not set up their tent on the edge of a crater. They do not judge people emotionally, because they aren't aware of their emotions.

Shrinking Africa is not an emotional issue. It is a materialistic concern. Both Bob and Boyd have come to terms with African emotions. African emotions are dressed up at ceremonies. Africans prefer bright colors, the color of their emotions. On the east coast they commonly speak Swahili. Their day-to-day expressions preclude any expression that doesn't correspond to their emotions.

Quite possibly this isn't the correct procedure, Bob said to Boyd. It took a great effort to admit this. The superhuman effort it took had infused a fierce red into his face. Both men trusted each other. They did not count their bullets. Their trust is a communal trust commonly found in the bush. By now they've killed or crippled eighty elephants, thirty-five alligators, one hundred and forty-two rhinos, two egrets, one great blue heron, and thirty-seven men, mostly black. There are half a dozen or so exceptions, but mostly black. Bob bent over one exception and searched his pockets. The man bore a slight resemblance to one of the two men in the newspaper clipping.

Ever since childhood the African theme, or at any rate, one of its many themes had struck a responsive chord in their hearts and minds. Everything that has happened on this continent, the fantastic sunsets, the howling hyenas, the dried elephant blood on the trail, the telltale sign of smoke, the bribes of gold dust, the poisoned darts, all had been anticipated by both men long before they came here.

Gradually they are approaching the Queendom of Quat. Gradually they are approaching the island off the east coast. They pass through settlements, and Africans seeing them hastily scratch curious signs, elaborate signs into the dark moist earth. It is the only defense they have against the dreadful events that are bound to occur. Everyone, seeing them, anticipates the end. Instead they smile and pay for everything they buy. It proves how deceptive appearances can be. It is confusing for the Africans. But the black bourgeoisie smile knowingly . . .

In my book I describe Bob and Boyd as follows: The two of them are still at it, crisscrossing the terrain that is being changed day by day, as the people from Tanzania and Malawi come bearing trees and sections of low hills that are to be reassembled inland . . . At any rate the two men are perpetually on the move, always on the lookout for signs of smoke, for tire marks, for cigarette stubs, at night they take turns sleeping. The newspaper clipping in Bob's bush jacket is faded and torn. They are no longer certain of the identity of the two. To make certain, to erase any sort of doubt, they have killed half a dozen men so far. They do it rather efficiently. Genuinely regretting their mistakes, they proceed. They are eager to make amends, and send letters to the relatives of the deceased. Short notes containing terse sentences of regret, and quite possibly, although I'm not certain of this, they also enclose a few of the man's belongings. In that respect they are scrupulously honest. They are also farsighted, and therefore ask the man to take a short stroll. Pow. One single shot . . . They speak fifteen click languages, but their Swahili leaves a lot to be desired.

They know that Tadhiribi means to look for and search Tamba is to creep, crawl, or move slowly.

Tambavu is something hung over the chest, a charm or an amulet to protect one from danger.

Tangaza is to make known or publish.

Toshea is to be amazed, astounded or staggered.

Toma is to fuck.

On the island Alfred is compiling a list of his recent

errors, his gaffes, his blunders. He is looking for an explanation. Not an explanation for his being here. He knows the reason for that, and the reason for his being employed by the Consul, and the reason for his having bought a house, and the reason for the fried dog on the menu. No, it is the other reason, the painful reason for Alva's departure that he needs to know.

Although he and the French Consul have become friends, he still doesn't feel free to call on him at any hour of the day. He'd like to see the Consul and possibly Alva at the right time. But he finds it difficult to determine the right time. The remaining blacks on the island know more about the right time than he does. They have an incredible sense of timing. They take days to cover a short distance and arrive at the right time. People everywhere are greeting each other, indicating a pleasure at the encounter, and an appreciation at the correctness of the timing. Alfred thinks about the consulate. There are rooms inside he hasn't seen. He feels grateful to the Consul but at the same time resents the latter's stiffness and formality. He walks as far as the gates of the consulate. They are closed. All he has to do is open them. For some, he realizes, opening the gates can be a heaven-sent opportunity. How erroneous, how misleading.

S

SOMEDAY SOON I shall return, and so my mind is fully preoccupied, and people observing me cross a street, or sipping some hot broth, or looking distracted as I buy a ream of paper, are convinced my mind must be on something else. My decision regarding my eventual return has made me buy a ream of paper I didn't need, a paper I might add produced locally, and not made from long green cucumbers. I bought it because I became distracted, and because I engaged a couple of friendly clerks in a conversation about Africa. I could read disbelief on all faces. Paper made from cucumbers. Ha ha ha.

Queen Quat confided in me: I like having a lot of power, and exerting it over others. Does it explain her country's predicament? Does it explain her letter?

Dear A. Come back quickly before all is gone. Come back and enjoy our stunning sunsets. I have recruited a dozen new men for my palace guard. All are six-footers. Alex and Allen arrived here a few days ago. In my absence both are questioning my aides. I've persuaded Allen he should leave Alex. He confides in me . . . I intend giving each one a map of my shrinking Queendom. Come see me soon. Accept my royal affection. Quat.

Staring across at mainland Africa a French Consul discovers a certain change of color, and also another less discernable change, less distinct, less noticeable, still it did give him a start. Could Africa be receding, or is his island drifting away from Africa? Perhaps, he mused, his eyesight is failing. Consequently all distances appear as even more distant. Could be. He checked his eyesight. It is first rate. He checked his pulse. First rate. He checks his eyes again by peering into the adjacent room, observing both Alva and his loved one entangled in a familiar routine of love, combining head and legs, but all a bit mechanical, a bit staged, a bit fake, he decides.

His loved one, her bleached blonde hair disheveled, enters his room, asking: did I please my darling, and he lifting his head from his paperwork, from his consular duties, replies: my little cabbage could have been a bit more spontaneous, more relaxed perhaps . . . As a result of his criticism she sulks all evening.

Alva considers her options. She can remain or she can leave. Finally she opts for staying because she likes breakfast in bed.

Both Alex and Allen have covered a lot of ground since leaving Queen Quat. Most of it is level ground inhabited by ants. Both have negotiated for each step forward, paying ants in sugar. By now both have glazed eyes and no longer remember certain Swahili speech sounds, such as Sabili . . .

Sabili is an obstacle

Safihi is arrogant

Saka is hunting animals

and Miti Safu Safu is a line of trees

and Sahau is forget

and Shauku is sexual passion

and Shaua is excitement and desire, especially desire not gratified

and Shamili is an ear ornament

and Sheshe is beautiful

99

and Singiza means insinuate

and Susuika means keep asking and asking, and simultaneously applying a bit of pressure

and Suta means making charges openly

Alfred has an incomplete inventory of seven hundred pages. It enables him to pinpoint Alva's approximate location in the consulate. Queen Quat, however, relies chiefly on her drums, her constantly beating drums. Although she doesn't doubt drum's accuracy, she complains a lot. She keeps saying:

Same shit same scenery same suffering saints same soup same spiel same safaris same safeguards same saffron sauce same sailboats same salads same salamis same saliva same salesmen same salutations same samples same sanctimonious shit same sanctuaries same sandals same sandbox same sandstorms same sangfroid same sanitary shit same sapphires same sapphism same sardines same savages same sawfish same sayings same scandals same scavengers same scents same schisms same schools same scrawls same sculpture same seasons same seclusions same secrecy same secretions same sects same seditions same seeds same seizures same self same semicircles same sensibility same sentences same sensations same servants same servings same sex same sharks same sultans same shells same shipwrecks same shocks same shots same shamanism same shrill shrieks same shouts same sights same signifiers same sites same situations same sixth sense same skeletons same skepticism same skirts same skills same slaves same sleep same sleeping sickness same slaughter same smoke same smooth surface same smut same snakes same snapshots same sneers same social scenes same studies same solar system same soldiers same SOS same searching same space same sparks same spears same spirit same sphincter same spirals same spiders same staged shows same standstills same statements same stench same stealth same stations same stays same stability same stiffness same stonework same storehouses same storms same stories same silhouettes same sheep same semi-precious stones same shelters same squares same stamps same stanzas same stares same starfish same starts same sterility same stratums same streams same streets same strengths same stubborn streaks same stuff same styles same subdivisions same sublime summer same submerged submarine same suction same Sudanese same suffering same sugar same suggestions same suicides same suits same summarizations same summits same summons same sunshine same sunstroke same supernatural same supper same supplies same suppositions same serpentine steps same separations same sequestrations same shit same suppressions same supremacy same surplus same surroundings same surtax same survivors same suspects same suspense same Swahili swallows same swans same swaps same swarms same swarthy Swazis same sweat same sweep same sweetheart same sworn statements same swinging symbols same swordsplay same syllables same syllogisms same symbiosis same symmetry same sympathy same symphony same symptoms same syntax same souvenirs same spectrum same speculations same sporadic sprees same staples same steatopygia same sterilized syringes same surprises.

R

READING IS a most rewarding exercise, claims Jacqueline. Jacqueline is an impatient reader, always hastily running her eyes down a page, always looking for a particularly eventful passage, and consequently Jacqueline misses a description of Alva on page forty-nine and on page ninety-nine. Like most people, Jacqueline reads chiefly for amusement, and draws her own conclusions about certain less amusing incidents, for instance incidents in my own life, and by disregarding certain descriptions of interiors, her brain keeps omitting page after page of conversations, not realizing, perhaps, how much one can miss by missing a remark made by Queen Quat: I regret not having more power over people. Moreover, after carelessly perusing my books, Jacqueline doesn't even retain a faint memory of how I became obsessed by an incredible fear of being crushed alive by a mad elephant. I despair as her eyes jump back and forth. Jacqueline is reading aloud from my book, and for Alva's benefit, adding a few comments of her own. He's a real prick . . . a real opinionated prick.

Possibly Alva replies: I knew him once. He gave me five hundred dollars. I could easily have asked for more. He double-crossed Alex and Allen. He had convinced me how easily Nicholas could be kidnapped for a ransom. A pushover, he called it. Alex and Allen believed everything. Instead,

Nicholas fought like a madman. Alex killed him. Quat and I got rid of Nicholas's body. Inadvertently I must have helped Quat obtain Nicholas's briefcase containing his African collection. All along I had fed Alex and Allen false information. I believed everything I heard. Everything.

Alfred also reads my books. Restlessly he is placing my existence in an inventory. Being indiscriminate, his inventory also includes Rimbaud in Aden evadin‿ or escaping from European pricks after being raped on a boat by its crew. Daily he's asked by a French Consul how is he progressing.

Reading is a most rewarding exercise. One can learn a lot from books. I informed Queen Quat how reading my books could open new horizons for her, and even provide guidance, if guidance is ever needed. I like having power over people, Quat remarked.

Ants have identical problems, I replied.

Quat believes in reading and avariciously reads books, palms, faces, gestures, drum beats, hoofprints, footprints leading from an adjacent island, a particular island. Her attention is always focused, no, it is riveted on one island. Information reaches her about Alfred's inventory, his eclectic and inaccurate inventory. Day by day her curiosity keeps growing. Her boundless curiosity encompasses not only Alfred, but also Alva and Jacqueline and her husband. Does he mention me in his inventory, Queen Quat keeps asking everyone. Does he?

Each day Queen Quat loses a bit more property, a few more cliffs and grasslands and mountains and rocks and paved roads. From her personal perspective it appears as if a certain island is drifting away from her country. A certain process of disassociation may result. How regrettable. Meanwhile her country is becoming more and more crowded as more and more people move into each remaining acre of land, and fewer buckets of orange paint are being requested by her painters, as people crowd into each other's houses and into each other's beds, occasionally a dozen living in a hut, enjoying each other's proximity in bed.

Queen Quat has found ruling a delightful experience. One can learn a lot from ruling people, from dominating people, from pushing rebels into detention camps. Her present priorities are, first, introducing order and color and greatness and honor and certain amusements. I'm not really concerned about fame, Queen Quat asserts modestly. I demand glory, but glory is posthumous. Because Her Majesty has been losing a bit of property lately, her Corps of Engineers proposes a night assault on a certain adjacent island. Had Alfred's inventory been available many needless headaches and arguments might have been alleviated.

I'd like a revolutionary reception, Queen Quat decides. But most revolutions in Africa follow an innate cycle: all revolutions being closely followed by an antirevolution and none of Her Majesty's advisers knew if an attack on a certain island might just find all antirevolutionary forces in power. I'd prefer a revolutionary reception, if at all possible. I'd prefer a group of humble guerrilla fighters assembled at my HQ after having requested my intervention against . . . but here Her Majesty pauses, being at a loss, not knowing if an antirevolutionary or a revolutionary force is in power. Her aides dash back and forth, into and out of her library, reading reference books, consulting documents. Even her personal correspondence is perused. Her red-faced aides finally admit, history is in her hands. Quite, remarks Quat drily. I'll march on a certain island. It is her first invasion. Like all first invasions it is a bit awkward, a bit amateurish. For instance all painters are recruited and given a four-hour course in forming a human bridge . . . all are given flotation collars, and are linked by an endless metal cable . . . My painters' courage enabled my army . . . etc., etc., claimed Her Majesty afterward. My country owes my painters a great debt of gratitude . . . Hip hip hurray, her army cried as one man. And afterward: For she's a jolly good fellow, for she's a jolly good fellow . . .

But regrets are not easily abandoned. Regrets are not easily disguised. Regrets blossom in a hot climate, blossom early each morning. I have no regrets, claims Alfred. None at all. I left Europe free of regrets. I left, closely following Rimbaud's instructions. I left after an amazing, an incredible encounter in a locker room. As I left I composed a poem about not having any particular feeling of regret. And now, if I at all regretted Alva's departure I'd be circling a certain French consulate daily. However, aimlessly circling a large building might only impede my inventory. It might also damage my health . . .

Although Alfred compulsively keeps circling a French consulate, it hasn't affected his health. Exercise is good for one's health. A French Consul observes Alfred circling his building, and remarks: Bizarre, quite bizarre. Alfred circles a particular building on an average of fifteen circles an hour. As he circles around and around he hopes he'll locate Alva, or at least catch a glimpse of her. If a French Consul hadn't focused his attention at Alfred, no one might have noticed him, because he's a pretty inconspicuous kind of guy.

Because a French Consul keeps observing Alfred, all day long keeps his eyes focused on a lone figure of a man circling a large building at a rate of fifteen circles an hour or approximately one circle every four minutes, he doesn't observe

105

Queen Quat's Corps of Engineers constructing a human bridge, although if he had only raised his head a bit he'd have caught Quat's army crossing a human bridge, crossing a long chain of former painters, all desperately avoiding death by drowning. For her invasion Quat had her army learn a few elementary phrases . . . and now, crossing a human bridge, each fresh recruit recites aloud . . .

Ramia is a bullet

Rewa is a large drum

Rula is a ruler, an instrument for measuring distance

Randa is a dance of men, a dance revealing courage

Ratibu means, arrange, or put in order

Preceding her invasion Queen Quat holds a ruler and measures a map of her diminishing Queendom. It is a disheartening experience. For good measure Quat also measures herself, and regaining her confidence, practices measuring her palace rooms and her favorite aides, ah ha . . . Quat finds measuring quite exciting, and carried away, continues measuring doors, and archways, but experiences a certain difficulty measuring fallen arches . . . Finally Quat measures her palace guards. Attention. All fifty at attention are being measured. If Alfred only knew. It might make his inventory a bit more interesting. Doubtlessly he'd enjoy a measuring experience. All he'd need is a little ruler . . . pronounced rula. Everyone in Queen Quat's presence nods and grins, anticipating miracles from a rula . . .

I am a rula, announces Queen Quat and everyone flattens himself in front of her Majestic feet.

Down, down . . . and all are face down.

If I measure downward I find no diminution, declares Queen Quat. My greatest loss exists if I go outdoors and measure lengthwise. Poor Quat. Her loss is Africa's loss.

106

Q

QUOTATIONS FROM an African Chairman of History: An African historian's memory is as long and as durable as his pencil, manufactured in England, France, America, Belgium, Portugal, Italy or Germany. In point of fact an African historian's memory gradually decreases as he purposefully jots down a historical analysis of pencil manufacturing. Like everyone else, a historian has his preferences. He might prefer English pencils instead of French ones. However, by and large, an African historian's preferences are immaterial. In Africa a historian is largely a bookkeeper. He prides himself on knowing past annual exports of carved African figures, a lively business, and also current figures for pencils imported annually from Europe and America, and number of missionaries arriving daily carrying pencils in one or another pocket, pencils for jotting down appropriate figures for divine intervention.

A day before Queen Quat's impetuous invasion of an adjacent island, a famous French newspaper carried following headline: Quat is a Queer Queen. But newspaper is promptly censored. One of its editors is imprisoned, but newspaper appears next day after making a minor deletion, although it doesn't change article in dispute, leaving in all mention of Her Highness measuring her guards.

Another long letter from Queen Quat. It is in her elegant hand. It is five feet long. It must have given our post office a great deal of difficulty. It may have given a few mailmen a letter nightmare. I open her letter. I notice at once her envelope is made of cucumber paper. Good old Quat. Not ashamed of buying African paper. I admire her loyalty, and ponder at her declared intention of invading an island because each day a group of men keeps making obscene gestures in her country's direction. How can I possibly overlook an obscene index finger held aloft in my direction, Queen Quat complains.

At dawn Queen Quat's army invades an adjacent island, crossing her live bridge of men, jumping from one bobbing head onto another. At least fifty men in her bridge drown instantly. All others desperately hold air in lungs, as Her Majesty's army arrives and assaults island's forces. Disappointingly enough, her army meets little opposition. Island's harbor and central market fall first. Fall easily. Eventually a jubilant population is organized for Queen Quat's ceremonial appearance. A day later Quat's army intelligence confiscates Alfred's incomplete inventory. Quat's aides check off everything in her possession. In one of Quat's many forests a drum announces latest figures exceeding one million men, animals, huts, cities, et cetera, being captured. Of course, most announcements are a bit exaggerated. But opposing forces are incredibly naive and believe every drum beat. One million is an incredible number. It means imminent collapse. Only African driver ants are holding out. Incredible ants.

In her five-foot letter Queen Quat had desired information from me about French consulate interior. Had asked for precise layout. Preferably maps indicating best entry. Naturally, Alfred has been grilled, and compliantly blurts out everything he knows about a certain consulate. Not having a good head for layouts he instead describes a French Consul's massive forehead, his large nose, protruding chin, pointed ears . . .

Imprisoned by Queen Quat, he doesn't miss Alva as much as he expected, and claims philosophically: man experiments in his loneliness.

He's full of bullshit, asserts Queen Quat.

Now her generals, having made a few quick decisions, are cutting island's easternmost part into four equal parts. Carrying bazookas, mortars, automatic antiant devices, Quat's army continues its lightning advance, as ants fall back in despair, burning ant bridges, ant cuneiform codes. Exuding confidence, Quat marks freshly captured anthills on her map. Now, if only Alfred could describe consulate's interior.

Let's go over it again, Quat orders Alfred.

Having been impressed by consulate furniture, he lovingly describes another ornately carved desk.

Quat's aide hits him on bridge of his nose. He bleeds heavily. Everyone in Alfred's cell is embarrassed by his profusely bleeding nose. All look away as Alfred haltingly describes an interior of a French consulate. Naturally it is all pure fiction. But if he'll keep on inventing, eventually, insists Quat's aide, he'll provide an accurate description.

Having arrived here a few days ago, both Bob and Boyd are observing Quat's invasion from inside a French consulate. Both consider Consul a decent guy. Just as consulate is being encircled, Bob and Boyd are enjoying a finger-licking meal. It is a barbecued dog. A personal pet, Consul had assured both. Discovering Quat's army outside consulate's front entrance, both Bob and Boyd keep an icy calm.

Pass another leg, Bob grunts.

Magnificent men, decides a French Consul.

Barbecuing makes a big difference, claims Bob, licking his fingers.

P

PEN OR PENCIL AND PAPER allow one a completely objective portrayal of an African debacle. I personally prefer a paper made from pulp containing cotton fibers. I don't care for lined or colored paper. I also prefer paper made in large paper mills. I always order a minimum of one hundred pounds. After all, I am a prolific author. I find paper is ideal for documenting far-fetched invasions, invasions including annihilation of one million ants, antelopes and alligators. Personally I possess precious little information about Her Majesty's invasion, except for an occasional letter from her, and an occasional news briefing. However I do know how a certain French Consul photographed his building for insurance purposes. He has already filled in all necessary papers. After lovingly photographing each interior, he closes a door. It is almost a final leave-taking. All of Africa is presciently aware of each move he makes. All of East Africa follows his movement on drums. He moves down a consular corridor locking one door after another. Finally he develops and prints his film in a basement darkroom, and is disconcerted as he discovers Bob and Boyd in his 11×14 enlargements. It is monstrous, he decides. How did both Bob and Boyd creep into his enlargements. But because both female faces are coyly averted, he can't decide if one could be his Jaqueline . . . He examines each photograph carefully. He finds it difficult drawing any conclusion . . . He has been preoccupied by his

110

insurance problems and never noticed if any beds in his bedrooms had been occupied. Perhaps it is his imagination. Could he possibly be falsely attributing . . . could he be erroneously attributing an obscene and perverse act . . . could he be . . . No. He doesn't attribute anything. He merely examines a few photographs. Her identity isn't at all certain. Even her nose is dissimilar. As for her companion. Ha . . . all of her face is obscured by a man's back.

African drums frantically beat out message, asking: is it conceivable behind a female face lies a man's face. Africans love an inquiry into love, especially on a consular level.

French Consul adjusts enlarger's lens, and prints photographs of his joyous oblivion.

At night a couple of men emerge from a French consulate. Both are in camouflaged overalls, and both are carrying a canvas bag containing eighty pounds of dynamite, and holding a forty-five in one hand as both crawl in an easterly direction past a few guards. By midnight both have located a human bridge, at least have heard parts of it chatting in an East African dialect, concluding: Ah ha, bridge ahead. In one and a half hours Bob and Boyd attached dynamite at fifty foot intervals, as parts of human bridge are falling asleep. At one forty-five Bob presses a plunger, and . . . Pow . . . Boom . . . Pow pow . . . Boom an East African night is briefly illuminated by a number of explosions. In one moment all invading forces have been deprived of a means of getting out fast. In one blow all mainland avenues are closed. Now Her Highness can't get any fresh provisions, not even cucumber paper for her plans. In one night everything has changed.

Crawling back on all fours, Bob and Boyd are challenged by an armed guard. Password, he calls out in a foreign dialect. Bob is convinced it has a P in it. He hazards a few guesses.

111

Pale-e-e-e, meaning a great distance, and

Pambasua maneno, meaning, making a case clear, and

Penya, meaning, penetrate, get inside, enter, but also implying it is a bit difficult, and

Pindua, meaning, give a different direction, and

Pumba, meaning, one is incapable of an answer because of one's astonishment, and a patient guard finally becomes irate and fires a burst in Bob's direction.

Piss off, bawls Bob furiously, and guard meekly answers: OK buddy . . .

I knew it, Bob exultantly informs Boyd. I knew first letter of password is a P. P as in prick.

On following day Her Highness enters island's forest on foot. An hour later drums mysteriously become quiet, and all Africans intuitively know a great leader has disappeared. All mourn her passing as on fifth day of invasion French airplanes fly overhead and drop bombs on central market and on consulate by mistake. A dreadful error has been committed. Afterward all islanders attend a mass funeral, collecting arms, legs, heads and mutilated bodies . . . Alfred is immediately freed and put in charge of funeral inventory. He oversees all burial details, insisting on each coffin containing at least one head, one pair of legs, one pair of arms and one body. Admiringly a few Africans observe him as he numbers each arm and leg as if his life depended on it. How can our country ever defeat men like him, one man finally admits. He is numbering our arms and legs . . . But a pedantic man can easily be defeated, another man answers, if one deprives him of his numbers. All Africans burst out laughing.

O

ONE IS ALWAYS either moving forward or back-
ward, one is always carefully considering different alternatives,
one is always driven by insane but meticulously considered
needs, one is always buying objects in bags cr in boxes for
future consumption. One is also always carefully guarding one's
future. All of Europe is concerned about future considerations.
For instance, genius in Europe means a discerning anticipation of future needs. As he contemplated his future East African
invasion, Mussolini asserted, genius is genitals. Africans do
not need genius, because African concept of future is cloudy.
Africans have balls not genitals.

Now it is all over for her. Her majestic figure has been
obliterated from her country's consciousness, and East Africa
has erased her name from its annals, its monuments, its bridges
and avenues. It is a glorious majestic end as her black-draped
figure disappears forever in a large forest. All drum beating
has ceased, as if no further communication is now needed.
How easily African history is buried beneath a new contentment, a new impermanent joy. I knew her briefly. I accepted a
few ornaments from her in exchange for my not making known
her complicity in a murder of a jeweler in Antibes. I am
looking at her obituary in a French newspaper. Most of it is
misleading, most of it is false.

Having moved again from one modern air-conditioned

apartment building in Antibes into another almost identical building, and looking out and finding in front of me an almost identical landscape, almost East African in its incredibly lush green beauty, almost moving as its flickering lights dance in front of my eyes, I decided I could, although I missed Africa, conduct my future African jaunt in a more leisurely manner from here by investing a few dollars each month in East African land, buying large areas of East Africa, eventually buying a country for myself. In my mind I am already going back and being greeted by drums and chimpanzee carnivals. In my mind I am once again embracing Alva. I have never abandoned her. I've had a few lapses, a few lapses of memory. Not deliberate lapses. Other events for a brief moment, four or five minutes at most, obscured my love for her. I can't ever forget how during my journeys in East Africa I had been greatly excited by constant drum beats informing everyone of my imminent arrival elsewhere, and how everyone I met asked me about my friendship, my inexplicable affection for Her late Majesty. In all candor, I must admit I envied her majestic carriage, her majestic motions, her majestic bearing. I believed her capable of invading all adjacent islands, capable indeed of capturing all of East Africa, and eventually all of Africa, and coloring an entire continent orange, her favorite color. But if genius is indeed genitals, her genitals didn't behave correctly, a misfunction of a certain kind, a minor disturbance, easily corrected by a few injections of elephant hormones. Once I believed my future depended on hers. Now my future depends on my completing my complete oeuvres, and on my investments in Africa. I invest heavily. I buy a former mansion, I buy a few forests, I buy as only a European can buy, out of consideration for my future needs.

If I am ever asked how I could erase history, I can answer at once. It's easy. I bought an eraser. After carefully choosing

114

an East African dictionary, I began by erasing a few phrases. I didn't erase everything I didn't like. I left a few lines for future historians. I left:

Ofisa, meaning officer as articulated by a native, and

Oga, meaning cowardly, nervous, easily frightened, and

Oleza kitu na kitu kingine, meaning, making one object like another, and

Ombwe, meaning an edge or a brink, and

Oradha, meaning a list, inventory, catalogue or invoice, and

Ota, meaning a dream, or have a dream, or being half awake, and

Oza, meaning corrupt, or go bad.

N

NOW A MASSIVE IRON GATE blocks everyone's entry, bars everyone from exploring among many consular debris layers, a charcoaled history about former African diplomatic events and functions, and furtive diplomatic diamond exchanges and lavish dinners and discreet arrangements following dinner between beautiful blonde ladies and gentlemen in black attire, ahhh. By now a massive iron gate is deeply embedded in a communal East African memory. Gate appears locked, but looking in between bars at a former French consulate, a former center of gracious living can be detected. News concerning burning and looting isn't available. By contrast news about ant extermination is much more detailed. All Africans enjoy a good laugh. Everyone enjoys an ant hors d'oeuvre. But as news finally is disseminated, more and more islanders gather at consulate's massive and monumental gates. Hoping for a lucky break, more and more men join fire fighters, and help extract a few burnt bodies and a few lovely gilded chairs, a few damp carpets, a large chandelier, a few gray metal file cabinets containing discriminating details concerning ant extermination and Her late Majesty's confusing genitalia. However, most dossiers are almost illegible. Besides, islanders are chiefly interested in furniture, and deliriously await gifts as chair legs and consular bric-a-brac, including heavy keys, are impartially distributed. Keys are immediately converted into amulets. Each key dangling between bouncing breasts as all dance and celebrate consulate's destruction.

A five-foot-long letter from Ndola conveys news about a French Consul, and his beloved Jacqueline, and her close friend Alva, fleeing from an island near Africa's east coast. Accompanied by a few hundred carriers, Consul, having lost his invaluable compass, leads everyone astray. However, he doesn't admit it. Eratically moving back and forth, he keeps consulting his map. History hasn't forsaken him. He is marching in front. Alva and Jacqueline are being carried in comfortable chairs far behind. Frequently both ends of caravan are miles apart. Consequently, after a few months, certain linquistic difficulties arise as both ends, having developed different dialects, can no longer communicate. It is most distressing. Lacking a compass, a dictionary and now, also a common memory, both ends are apprehensive about future contacts. Despondently, each morning French Consul holds a conference. Every inch a diplomat, he addresses his end, but he also is addressing a communal conscience of East and Central Africa. He keeps explaining in his aristocratic French how much he loves Africa. He knows Africans are easily moved by an emotional appeal. Africans, it appears, are moved less by explanations and more by eloquent facial expressions. French Consul, after all, is a master at conveying his distress by lifting an eyebrow. How delightful, how exquisite. African drums immediately describe facial expression. Consul is a consummate artist. Nobody can forget his fantastic expression. Everyone is lifting an eyebrow, enraptured at finding a new feat in communication. Arched eyebrows are included in a cuneiform code. I may be lost forever, comments French Consul, but I feel happy at having fathered a cultural explosion.

M

MAKING MEMORY MORE MEANINGFUL in darkest Africa, a certain Chief Auwik measures all meaning in his former life. By measuring his life he is clarifying his Europeanized morbidity. For him measurements have become a means for memorizing his former days at Eton. Marvelous and lovely days. Back in East Africa, he finds himself eating crickets again. However each meal evokes a deep and meaningful memory about former days. He and his close adviser, a former missionary, a Bach loving man, make much ado about beatific days at Eton. Ahhh, glorious carefree days, eating chocolate fudge and caning fags in dormitory. Ahhh, beatific. Appalled by his great country's backwardness, Chief Auwik, basically a loving man, introduces life measurements as an antidote against disguised colonialist elements in his country. At his insistence, everyone between eighteen and eighty, his immediate family included, must measure all meaning in life. As expected, everyone kept asking himself, how do I measure myself exclusively, if everything I do is being duplicated by everyone else. Consequently, everyone is largely detached and indifferent during measurements . . . although, at Chief Auwik's insistence, measuring frequently entails hunting for a man in Central Africa and bringing back his feet. For measuring life's meaning, East Africans draw an imaginary line inside each hut, and mark each line by burying a captured foot exactly beneath line. Frequently measurements are a bit bloody. After conclud-

118

ing measurement ceremony, each man encloses his Central African feet in a black funereal casket, approximately eighteen by eight by five inches in dimension. Each container is carefully concealed because it has become a coveted key for an invaluable map, and could if examined indicate a man's measured meaning and also foretell his future. Everyone knows foreign feet are being concealed beneath each hut, and each building, but its exact location isn't known, because concealment is an ancient African art. After all, Africans have even concealed large areas of Africa by growing immense jungles and breeding crocodiles and alligators. Enclosed inside each casket are measurements indicating a man's height, length, and also his lovemaking ability, although allowances are made for mechanical breakdowns and for failures.

As a great African continent is gradually decreasing and crumbling at its edges, buried black caskets are becoming more and more meaningful. Each day more and more men cross into Central Africa looking for feet. Each evening at least fifteen hundred men are drawing imaginary lines. Field Marshal Awery, Chief Auwik's cousin, has composed a jolly African ditty:

> Hold a Central measure, and
> Discover a meaningful leisure,
> La la
> La la.

Incidentally, after caskets containing feet become a collector's item, a museum in Manhattan displays a few caskets alongside magnificent African amulets and jewelry. Everyone asks: do Africans love an individual foot for itself? as a museum audience gazes in bewilderment at a foot, a dark muscular foot. How marvelous, how beautiful, how menacing.

119

L

LEAVING ANTIBES BY AIR, I calmly light another cigarette in an Air France jet, and let another bright and glorious day alleviate a constant gnawing anxiety I have about landing in Africa.

Lokolama lies approximately eighty kilometers east from Lake Leopold, about a fast hour's drive from Lokolama airport, if I can drive at eighty kilometers an hour. Anyhow, I expect I'll be arriving at Hotel Cabral by five. Lokolama's airport, I discover, is an efficient and attractive airport designed by a French company. After landing I enter a large gleaming glass building. Apparently I am being expected at Lokolama's Great African Letter Auction, a clerk behind an airline counter explains. I find it amusing. I am actually being expected. In fact drums from a close-by jungle beat faster as I drive away in a jeep. I assume drums are informing auctioneers at auction hall how I am handling jeep, and how I look: composed, earnest, eager, handsome and immensely capable. Drums also describe leather luggage containing dollars in large denominations. Evidently Great African Letter Auction is a big event in Lokolama. Banners across highways announce letter auction, giving auction's exact location, and also listing a few important letters including a few I had lost. A few banners also carry advertisements for hotels, for bathhouses, and lists four individuals in

Lokolama, all former British agents and all extremely competent at deciphering illegible documents and letters.

Like everyone else deeply interested in letters I got a hand-engraved invitation for a Letter Auction in late July. Daily I had been complaining how I had been losing a few letters each day. I couldn't explain it. At first I didn't inform anyone about it, but after I contacted a few friends in early June I discovered how everyone else also interested in language and letters had been burglarized, chiefly and almost exclusively losing letters concerning Africa. Later I learnt how everyone believed I had a hand in all letter disappearances because I had always been interested in Africa. It helps explain everyone's erratic behavior, and everyone's coolness. How infuriating.

In losing letter after letter I had lost an entire African legacy including invaluable diagrams and cuneiform code books. How could I ever complete a book about Alva. I believe if I hadn't got an invitation, I'd have invented an excuse for coming back here.

Confidently I arrive at auction, and enter large hall, greeting a few attendants, all grinning knowingly because all has been arranged beforehand. A few less important letters have already been bought. I don't hesitate. Lifting an eyebrow I bid another five hundred and another hundred. In an hour I have bought four incredibly intimate letters, fifteen erotic letters, five doubtful letters containing a few forged lines, eleven love letters from Her Highness, also a few incriminating letters from Bob and Boyd I had lost. Afterward I cable a few friends in Antibes: Everything accomplished. Back in a few days. Letters haven't aged a bit. Best. A.

Later, having explored Lokolama's dense downtown district, I decided against dinner at hotel, and instead ate at a

French bistro, and afterward, feeling I could afford a little celebration, feeling I could blow fifty bucks, I asked a hotel bellboy for a chick. He immediately consulted his black book, asking if I'd like a black chick, a blonde chick. I handed him a drawing. It is a familiar drawing depicting a female knee and a female elbow. I explained I'd like a chick having a knee and an elbow like knee and elbow I had drawn. He examined drawing carefully.

An hour later I'm in bed kissing a chick. I hadn't expected a duplicate Alva. I hadn't anticipated a female impersonating Alva. Every gesture, every expression! I feel deliriously happy. I kiss her gently, and as I do I feel a gigantic heart inside another body beat like a distant drum. But despite everything, despite love, generosity, heartbeats and fantastic eagerness, I carefully lock all doors.

But baby, I hear her ask, how can I leave afterward?

I kept dreaming about Alva. But as I awake I discover I'm alone in bed. I knew it. I just knew it. Briefcase containing all letters is gone, and all cash except for fifty bucks I always keep in a boot. How can I go back emptyhanded. I desperately cable a friend for cash. I keep hoping he'll answer as I lie in bed feeling as if I had been hit by an avalanche.

Bellboy kindly explains, Laghai in East African dialect is, cheating, deceiving, beguiling . . . also Laika is downy hair, Ahhh, and Launi is likeness, and Lewa is being intoxicated, and Lumbwi is a chameleon.

K

KNOWLEDGE DERIVED FROM BOOKS hardly ever improves killing efficiency because even illustrated books containing diagrams aren't as instructive, as deadly, as calculating, as desperate as an actual experience in bush, in jungle, deep in any African interior, aren't as capable as a human hand as it grips a knife in its five fingers. Books cannot accurately direct a knife into another body except in a generalized diagrammatically anatomical fashion. Books, however, can explain almost everything, including how a four-inch folding knife can cut an artery, and how all bodies collapse inwardly as a knife is inserted. But actually finding a correct area in a body for a knife isn't at all easy, because bodies aren't immobile, because bodies aren't diagrams in books. Like everything else, experience doesn't come easily at first. Certainly books don't describe intense excitement as an assailant flashes a knife, and how each body gravely accepts a knife's cutting edge as a brief interloper, instantly adjusting itself, instantly concealing its hatred in a forced forgetfulness, as it drifts away, as it grasps air in its fingers, allowing its hard guest, its intruder a fine door into its heated interior. A body accepts its changes, accepts a briefly dislocated heartbeat, as blankets and hot frenzied hopes fight a coldness. Finally it conceals all hope for life by imitating a diagram from a book, as if by joining in a disastrous kinship, it can alter a historical evidence. But, I admit, a few inept assailants derive all knowledge from books, and begin each day by exercising all five fingers as if each hand is an instrument. Inept assailants are easily detected, because invariably all are burdened by a book, frequently confusing it for a knife.

J

JUST ANOTHER ANT INVASION, claims Jubutu, an African assistant auctioneer, as buildings all around collapse and crumble, creating great dust clouds. As can be expected, everyone in Jada is fleeing, carrying belongings in boxes and crates, carrying babies and clocks, carrying everything conceivable, everything but books about driver ants, Africa's ferocious ant. I've been informed driver ants are advancing at about forty feet an hour, but gradually, even at forty feet an hour, an entire city is invaded, and completely demolished as ants enter each building, conducting a floor by floor exploration, eating a few banisters, a few floors, a few beams. I had come here hoping I'd find Alva, hoping I'd come across evidence confirming everything I have claimed in a few books about her. Admittedly, by joining Alex and Allen, Alva has disproved a certain book's accuracy. I'm distressed, but I'm far from being disheartened. I can always begin again, from beginning, from initial chapter, from Antibes. I do admit Alva, if Jubutu's descriptions are correct, has completely disproved a few crucial facts, but facts can always be changed, can always be adjusted, can always be altered.

Just ants, explains Jubutu casually, as I hear a creak, followed by a great crunch as a ceiling comes down, enveloping everyone inside bedroom in dust. I had just been hoping I could attend another good auction. It could have compensated for a former disaster. I had been informed by Jubutu how he had a dozen African handwritten journals for auction, including Alex's I discovered. Great. Fantastic. I'll come. But after ants attack, auction is canceled. Apparently driver ants eat everything halfway edible. Goddamn . . . But am not alone in feeling despondent about cancellation. Jubutu is also despondent. He blames himself. He apologizes. He introduces his girlfriend. He's a big handsome guy. Dark hair, dark complexion, above average height, always joking. I bought him a drink and explained how I had innocently invited a chick, an innocuous gesture, and how everything, cash, briefcase, et cetera had disappeared . . . I had given her a hundred dollars . . . He just blamed himself again. Great guy . . Jubutu . . . great guy. But he couldn't, he explained, have an auction during an ant invasion.

He'd have continued if I hadn't hit him. I grabbed his bags and fled. His heavy but cheap bags. Both easily contain a dozen journals. Afterward I discover eighteen journals. I had hit him impetuously. I had been hoping I'd get a glance, just a glance at a few journals. I'm especially curious about Alex's dubious journal. But I can't examine journals because ants are attacking from all directions.

Just breaking fresh ground, I explain, but hardly anyone gives a damn as I dig a large hole beneath a familiar-looking footprint I have discovered behind a former hotel in Jebba after it had been destroyed by driver ants. I arrived at Jebba at four, found familiar footprints at eight, dug a hole and exhumed a body. I believe it is Boyd's body. I'm almost certain . . . he's buried in his flashy boots and in his bush jacket. He has a few bullet holes in his chest and belly. I fear Alex did it. Both Alex and Allen.

Ants have completely cleaned a city. A few clean bodies

are blocking an entrance into an empty house, a few dead ants are caught between crushed beams. Everywhere houses are empty, deserted, abandoned, demolished. But after another few hours Jebba's citizens are back, building another city inside a former city. Everything is extremely efficient. A destroyed building becomes a church, another a funeral home, another an auction hall. Jubutu died from a concussion after a beam hit his head. I find all his journals engrossing. I inspect another journal as a hotel is being built inside a former hotel. After an hour I enter it and ask for a comfortable bedroom. Everything is a bit cramped, but I don't complain. I close a door and extract a journal, Alex's journal from Jubutu's briefcase. Finally . . .

Alex hasn't changed. He blames everyone else for his indescribable ineptness and idiocy. It's almost amusing. Even I am accused. Accused by him as having devised an incredible burglary, in fact, devised everything, because I had hoped he'd be caught. He also claimed I am jealous . . . because he, Allen and Alva believed in friendship, a friendship I couldn't ever comprehend, and also because both he and Allen, by having had Alva, had also attained a far distant happiness I hadn't ever had.

Alex and Allen left for Africa hoping I had forgotten everything, but I haven't. He claims I have always concealed all emotions, all hostility, all hatred beneath innocuous descriptions in books and beneath a calm face. I deny it completely.

I DENY HAVING CONCEALED any hostility, any hatred and divisiveness in a book I am completing about Alva. All attacks are easily disproved. I haven't ever considered distorting, dissembling and falsifying anything except for a few intimate details, colorful details in a double bed, but deletions, I assert, can't be considered falsifications despite Alva's accusations, and despite Alex's accusations, because I have always deleted in good faith, hoping I could find in completed book a far far distant happiness.

I admit I am, as everyone is, a captive, being held captive by certain ingrown habits. I believe I can explain how I as a child became a captive . . . having a father, a bright inventor, a capable energetic explorer, I became influenced by his inventions, his electric carpet, his dirt duplicator, his flying exhaust fan, his folding automobile, his collapsible building, his fog curtain hanger and his balanced head adjuster. How could his extraordinary inventions fail in improving existence, although I'm deeply dismayed by Africa's apathy and indifference as far as his incredible inventions are concerned. But father didn't care about his ideas being accepted. Goodnaturedly he dismisses all acclaim and accolades. He's busy, and he can't bother about confusing claims concerning Africa's continental drift. He doesn't even acknowledge basic differences between countries, especially black countries, considering all inhabitants equally beyond his comprehension. Consequently he hardly ever glances at a book, because implicit in almost all descriptions in a book are differences, frequently erroneous differences, because descriptions in books are building characters by adding and adding information, erroneous and frequently divisive information, he claimed. I admit I became confused by his harsh criticism. For instance he claims, differences in human beings are essentially design differences . . . Gender confuses all important issues. An instantaneous change could come about if everyone could accept his/her human body design. If genitalia is an issue, an inventor could easily invent an interchangeable devise, clean, hygienic and comfortable, eliminating gender altogether. His carpet, another invention, had a broadloom gender. Anyone could clean it. He disliked abstract ideas. He couldn't be bothered about Alva. He'd glance at a book about Alva and Alex and claim it isn't essential. I agreed. His criticism could hurt, but I'd agree. But am I accurate enough, I asked him. He frowned. He flung a book away because it didn't amuse him. He closed his door. I had almost been hurt by his door I decided. I almost had a finger caught in his door. He couldn't give a damn. Accurate enough, indeed. It is all coming back.

I don't dig into ground because everything, but everything is above, and by digging I am falsely implying an interior, a depth beneath. Interiors don't exist, only distances exist, and here in Africa distances are decreasing daily, consequently by a certain future date I expect I'll find a former friend, a fucking former friend. I haven't forgotten how it all began. I am alone, but I haven't forgotten how for a fun-filled briefly felt feeling I fitted into another body and concluded briefly how a great happiness had descended and entered each, each indolently holding each, as contortion after contortion confirmed both individual existences as also being existence. Consequently I concluded I am existing, and in existing found a freedom, a further freedom allowing innumerable escapades, allowing absolute floating awareness in drifting as existence. But how can I avoid feeling anything but exhaustion after having had considerable elated and elevated feelings, elevated by arms and feet, also elevated by an existential desire for feeling . . . anyhow, exhaustion creeps into body and brain, I contemplate another happiness arising in a book, for instance, a book can extend an existence, can communicate a happiness again and again, in each case anticipations becoming delineated against a dark continent . . . I don't deny, accusations can follow each bodily encounter. Alva astounded by a certain book, claims I distorted everything because I felt envious. Her criticism has been borrowed firsthand from a certain filing cabinet, a consular filing cabinet. I have heard her false facts before. I feel irate because her claims are irrelevant. But I have invited her attack by coming back and facing ferocious ants, and by giving her impersonator fifty dollars . . . as if I could have hoped fifty dollars could convince her, could instantly erase everything I have ever expressed in books about her . . . erase everything I had imagined I had done . . .

But I have forgotten everything. I have already forgotten
Alitoa idhini indicates, he gave his consent,
and
Ikoje implies an interrogation,
and
Ila is a defect, a blemish, a drawback, a disgrace, a blot,
and

Imara indicates a hardness,
Imla implies, dictation.

Eventually, I'm convinced every "I" imparts its intense experience before it is erased and immobilized in a book. Ahhh
. . . how fast it disappears. He is being deceitful, claims Alva.
Everytime I approach, he flees back into a book. He's afraid . . .

H
HUGE BLACK CLOUDS gather and dangerously hover above as a deliriously happy African audience attentively follows Alva's creative body contortions, Alva's eager fluttering gestures, Alva's foreign behavior, Alva's curious dramatic cries, as Alva bathes and dresses, and, between events, embraces Alex and Allen. Africans are enthusiastic and have entire cast, especially Alva, coming back for curtain calls.

Africans everywhere can hear drums describing Alva's conspicuous contours, a fetching body, attractive breasts, certain areas decreasing as Alva breathes, Ahhh, and her blonde hair, enchanting, a falling curtain hiding her facial expression as Alva astride Alex's body, astride Alex's erect cock, faces Allen's erection, as Allen approaches, having heard drums beat, and having concluded how her face beneath her blonde hair contains another equally hungry face . . . however her clear blue eyes are formed by a clear conscience.

All foreigners are actors for an African continent. All foreign bodies, hands, feet, belly, chest, breast, buttocks and heads are antennas for African emotions, African amusements. Africans hesitate a bit before coming forward and admiring bodies, carefully, cautiously caressing, as foreigners archly exclaim, Ahhh ahhh ahhh. Alva disconcerted by her curious audience hides herself behind her blonde hair, behind her blonde curtain, as an African extends a black arm. . .

132

Can an audience's enthusiasm demolish a house?

Conditions are changing constantly, but a cheerful and demanding audience can always change everything, especially a house.

Having bought a house in Hyrra Banda, having hung essential curtains and built closets and closed doors, both Alex and Allen cheerfully greet another day, cheerfully greet Alva, having forgotten former grudges and hostility, having forgotten and evidently forgiven everything, as all embrace another cheerful African day, but below, despite closed doors, despite gates and German guard dog, despite foreign evasiveness, despite foreign hardness, an audience has gathered and having forced gates, having choked dog's bark, and crossed English garden and entered closed door, beaming, grinning, because all foreigners are great actors, and all foreign complaints, for example: "All Africans are cannibals," are extremely funny.

Don't go downstairs!
Alex accepts Allen's broad hint. Accepts Allen's desperate gesture. Don't go downstairs because everyone's downstairs . . .
Everyone?
Absolutely everyone.
Having entered a dining area, admired furniture, everyone began cooking, baking actually, a German guard dog.

Another African drama comes home. Books about Africa are deceptive at best. Few authors are aware how a certain house at Hyrra Banda, having been built from a European eighteenth-century design, hasn't changed despite everything else changing, despite continuous arguments favoring change,

133

but changeless house contains a fashionable eighteenth-century English garden, an arched gateway, a bamboo bird cage, an empty doghouse, a brick chimney, a high hedge cut each fourteenth day. As expected, everyone admires house and hedge and chimney and comes away considering house a foreign drama, but definitely attractive, definitely enhancing Africa.

Considering Africa's gradual deterioration and Africa's decreasing area, a European house could easily become a dramatic focal center for foreign ceremonies. As all huts and African bush and gigantic forests drop away at edges, all European buildings, being better built, could form a future African environment, and following author's assumption, eventually another African future could dramatize Africa's European background.

At breakfast everyone curiously crowds around Alva, as Alva a bit dumbfounded by her audience, glances at a book entitled *How an African Breakfast Can Be Cooked Hurriedly for a Few Hundred Hungry Africans at 450 Degrees Fahrenheit.* How amazing, book claims certain ants are delicious. Choose eighty dozen beef ants . . . also Crême d'Ameisen . . . antipasto . . .

Have another bite.
Alex almost bites a feeding black hand. Alva hides behind her blonde curtain, but Africans aren't disconcerted. Amiably all eat breakfast . . . as Alex, Allen and Alva consider alternatives, consider escaping but daren't because a delicate balance exists between crumbling continent, curious African audience and an ant colony gnawing away beneath eighteenth-century building, a home away from home.

134

G

GROWING FORGETFUL, Alva forgot another appointment because Alva's appointment book borders at complete bedlam. After earmarking a, b, c, d, e, f, g, for future appointments, and also concealing all dates and addresses and candid comments from Alex and Allen, by encoding everything, Alva, alas, forgot code and can't decipher anything. Consequently, feeling desperate, blaming everyone else, Alva chucks bloody appointment book away. Alex and Allen being extremely alert, discover appointment book at garbage dump after five days. Both elatedly attempt deciphering Alva's code. After five days both are completely drained, because Alva's code can't be broken. Alva conceals everything behind a devious code, behind: abandon, abatement, abdomen, ability, able, abortion, abreast, abrupt, accelerate, accommodate, acock, adultery, adventure, affair, afternoon, agape, age, aggression, agreeable, ah, amateur, ambassador, amorous, anal, anatomy, ankle, anywhere, aroma, ass, atop, averse, back, balls, bare, batter, beat, bend, bite, block, blow, bush, clit, cock, come, contain, contract, coupling, crap, daily, embrace, erect, enjoy, entry, fetching, figure, fuck, give, gratify, graphically, guess . . . Alex complains about Alva always being furtive. Angrily both chuck book away and approaching Alva demand a certain compensation, after all, five days are blown deciphering Alva's bloody appointment book. But Alva's forgetfulness becomes an admirable and fitting defense against any compensation. Appointments, codes? asks blank-eyed Alva. Admittedly being extremely charming, albeit a bit arch, a bit fluttery and coy, but charming and also extremely feminine, Alva's forgetfulness becomes an acceptable asset. Both embrace and forgive Alva. But Alva's forgetfulness cannot be contained, becoming an African epidemic . . . as everyone becomes gripped by a formidable forgetfulness, gripped by a curious doubt concerning directions and a doubt about future behavior and a doubt about common customs, for example: customarily everyone greets a friend. Alex and Allen greet Alva each day. But both greetings cannot conceal a deep anxiety, although both carefully and deliberately exude a false gaiety, a fake assuredness about appropriate greeting: Good day Alva . . . Good evening Alva . . . Good-bye Alva . . . As both are fighting forgetfulness, both are also earmarking a better future, a future free from forgetfulness. But as forgetfulness envelops everyone, Alex even forgets direction from bathroom, but eventually Allen finds Alex, and both forgetting Alva's former anger, enter Alva's bedroom again, and become a captive audience for Alva's bitter denunciations. Alva complains about being another clit for Alex and Allen. But forgetfulness blissfully erases all her complaints from Alex's and Allen's brain, enabling both guys a buoyant ending for another buoyant fun-filled afternoon as both examine Alva's fantastic figure.

Forgetfulness even grips Ghana's famous glue factory, as feverish glue attendants boil animal fats and gingerly fill famous blue glue bottles, for gluing future envelopes, for a future generation. Alva buys a bottle for her correspondence, and finds a finger in her bottle. Ah, forgetfulness.

136

Gifted Europeans are always enriching Africa, claims Alex, as Allen carefully glues an envelope containing Alex's design for a glue gun. A good gun could effectively glue everything down. But Alva doesn't display any enthusiasm. Dejected Alex chucks envelope, claiming Africa doesn't deserve a further enrichment.

F

FANTASTIC CONCLUSIONS draw closer as carnivorous ants discover another dimension, a fourth dimension, and achieve an economical foothold along east coast. Also, after a brief African conquest, driver ants form an economical exchange, bartering enemy ants. At first a few Africans caution European and American capitalists against employing ants as easily as blacks, claiming efficiency at factories could drop, because ants could elude all control factors by being cleverly camouflaged . . . But even Alex concedes, ants devised and boosted an innovative design for communal existence. Bullshit, asserts Allen. Efficiency experts are easily confused by ants, although ants cannot even distinguish a bee from a butterfly.

But Alva can distinguish a distended dog's belly from a crocodile belly, because all crocodiles' bellies don't contain any colored condiments or buttons.

Fantastic conclusions draw closer as Africans discover further ant capabilities, and begin employing cheap ants for farms and factories, and also acquiring driver ants for breeding. Everyone claims ants are enriching Africa, as enriched Africans go around buying everything, and by buying asserting an enormous buying capacity . . . and consequently also asserting an enormous demand for bags. But factories didn't anticipate demands. Formerly bags had been a dime a dozen. A dime a

138

dozen! Bags being absolutely essential, factories begin buying dog carcasses and after adjusting assembly, astutely demonstrate a dog's belly can be beautifully decorated and become a fine bag. As demands create better and bigger dog belly bags, bag factories are built alongside butcher's association. Each day dogs become bags. Eventually even ants avoid dog entrails. Confounded dogs.

As could be expected, economists arriving from abroad examine fresh African buying capabilities, and also examine factories and ant farms. Apparently ants are extremely capable, and can also build fine Danish furniture. But economists cannot conceal disappointment after examining diminutive chairs. Can Africa ever export diminutive chairs. Economists consider export for ants abroad. An economist actually begins a book entitled: *Ants as Consumers.*

As forgetfulness drifts across entire city, a few Africans cannot find a certain avenue, also everyone appears a bit blank-eyed, carrying empty dog belly bags and empty but fancy crocodile belly bags and empty but delightfully decorated elephant belly bags, back and forth, feeling a bit fearful because contagious forgetfulness erased all former charts, and because bus drivers cannot face forgetfulness, or admit forgetfulness. Enormous crowds at a central bus depot are asking for directions, and for buses, especially for 5 and 15 and 51 and 85, but buses aren't arriving, because all drivers a bit desperately are closing eyes, fighting forgetfulness as each drives around entire city. Forgetting everything, a few drivers disclaim being drivers, disclaim everything, everything except an extremely erotic existence. As for Europeans, a few almost forget Africans, and express fresh fantasies fit for an Alpine excursion.

E

EVELYN ANGRILY EYES Alva's contours. Evelyn, a copy editor at Ethiopian Books Corporation enviously erases authors' excesses. Erases every ejaculation, despite an Ethiopian editor's dissent. Evelyn even erases every discreet but distinctly explicit erotic episode, despite black editor's conspicuous dissent. But Ethiopian editor, although aghast at deletions, distinctly at a disadvantage, because at Ethiopian Books Evelyn alone can correctly copy edit English copy, and despite Emperor's exhortations, chief editor and editor's assistants are confused by distinctions between A and E. For example: Better and Batter, Band and Bend, Best and Bast, Bad and Bed . . . Although Evelyn doesn't ever express any envy concerning Alva, her deletions are completely destroying author's and also Alva's expectations. Evelyn erases balls and balling as day after day Evelyn's boss compliantly accepts her corrections. Before book appears editor assures book buyers for Emperor, all deletions are explicit deletions. Ahhh. Everyone expectantly eyes deletions. Example below:

Alva enters a dark apartment, and despite a certain experience expresses astonishment as an Ethiopian architect embraces and (deleted) enters abruptly by compelling Alva (deleted) all exhausted as (deleted) before even closing a door, as Alva calls Alex, but confronted by another appendage (deleted) drops (deleted). Appealing (deleted) as an entire (deleted) carefully caressing and (deleted) as ever (deleted) expands and contortion after contortion demonstrates an explosive conclusion. Eventually, after another (deleted) emerges as a depleted and enervated (deleted) but Alva's cries aren't answered. Both (deleted) depart after breaking down Alva's (deleted) . . .

Although Ethiopian Emperor doesn't deny Evelyn's copy editing capabilities, Emperor admits being a bit disappointed by Evelyn's clean cuts. At an annual awards dinner Emperor after awarding Evelyn a classic educational award, expresses astonishment, because Evelyn decolleté didn't delete anything. All at dinner except Evelyn's chief editor, are enchanted. Ahhh. English deletions are beyond doubt an enormous achievement. Afterward Emperor educates Evelyn, explaining:

Ebu could be a contemptuous expression chiefly against children, and
EEeee! being an assent.
EEeee! exclaimed Evelyn.
and
Ekua could be a breaking down.
EEeee! exclaimed Evelyn.
and
Epa could be, avoiding danger.
EEeee! exclaimed Evelyn.

D

DRIVER ANTS are cleverly causing divisions between Africans, and causing concern among Africans at Central Bus Depot as buses don't arrive, as all discover avenues are blocked and certain bridges are collapsing, because ants are attacking after discovering Africa's diminishing continent can't contain all ants and all Africans. As ant attacks begin, Africans attempt deciphering ant communications, but ant code can't be broken. Alva calmly continues dressing, although all African armies are assembled at an airport, and danger appears certain. As Alva dresses, Alva also contemplates a delightful double dream. Alva's boyfriend can't decipher Alva's dreams because all dreams are basically a bit critical about boyfriend. Alva continues dressing dreamily, being absolutely devoid any apprehension. Boyfriend, disgusted by dreamy appearance, complains: come Alva . . . But Alva continues dreaming double dreams. Come Alva . . .

Am borrowing a car and driving away as another day abruptly appears, another beautiful day, but am convinced African continent actually being diminished and also causing anxiety amongst ants. Damned difficult driving because Africans are clinging and cajoling and begging because buses aren't arriving, and all are afraid, but am backing a bit backward, and Crash, Bammm, Boom, accidentally break a bus depot and also break a couple demanding clinging arms. A clear blue beautiful day as alligators and crocs betray an awareness concerning diminishment, because diminishing continent could also deprive all and cause devastation and banishment. Could be. As day advances ants darken bush. But am complacently driving along circuitous but charted bush, also dreaming a double dream about Alva, about arriving at Alva's apartment, but dreams can't close all divisions and can't correct distances. Cars can.

Am driving along as another daylight dresses bushes brightly, although cities are being abandoned after ants' designs are clearly determined, am driving curiously apathetic, curiously anesthetized, as bridge after bridge collapses.

Arriving at Dembidollo before dark, before driver ants can arrive. City appears abandoned. Am alarmed as beneath car a concealed driver ant attacks. Carefully crush ant. Damnation. Another clear day ceases as a continent diminishes by another bit. After consulting a convenient chart, am beating at a door, as another car, driven by an African, collides against close-by borrowed car, and after damaging an adjacent building crashes against a ditched bus. Clearly an appalling accident. Clearly an avoidable accident. Am beating at another door as an African driver is being chased by cops. Chase concludes as cops club driver. Am detached about driver dying. Apparently all cops carry clubs. Am convinced all data concerning clubbing can be deciphered by counting dead bodies after dark. But curiously clubs aren't an assured defense against ants. Cops avoid confrontation. As clubbed driver dies, am beating at another door, calling Alva, Alva . . . Am approached by a cop carrying a club. Cop demands a cash contribution . . . Annoyed am complaining about dead African driver as cop's club comes crashing down

143

against body . . . almost damaging damned arm. Arm aching, am driving away, blaming bloody ants, bloody continent. Am deeply disturbed by Alva's disappearance. Dangerous days. Discover city's central avenue blocked by cops and army behind barricades. Abandoning car, ably avoid all cops, as darkness covers another day's advance.

C

CUSTOMARILY AN AFRICAN CALENDAR begins as August brings a curious calm, almost an apathy amongst blacks, as all are convinced by ants' capabilities, convinced ants can conquer all coastal cities, and can also avoid being ambushed by army, because ants can build ant bridges alongside and beneath broken bridges. Am awed by clear blue above as all Africans are apathetically crouching, awaiting another brutal ant attack, although African armies could counterattack. But counterattacks are academic . . . because all are afraid. Am carrying binoculars, am consulting a chart as Africans assembled at city center brandish bows and arrows, crying: Awoooo, awoooo. A bloodcurdling cry. Am crossing a bleak coastal area. Am crossing alone by bicycle, by camel, by alligator cart, by boat, by black chanting carriers, by borrowed automobile, by bus, by buffalo, as black clouds above burst. Afterward an August calm covers all coastal areas. Am absorbed by carved artifacts chucked away among bushes by Africans as, am assuming, attacks began. Am admiring ancient coveted artifacts. Africans accept chaotic conditions, blaming corrupt army, badly built barricades, and confusing accents completely confounding communication between African countries. Artifacts are cheap and available, but can't buy any because boat's caboose already crowded, containing a bunk, a chair, a cuckoo clock, bookcase and books, clothing, cushions, bamboo curtains, cups, a clavichord, a boat crank, canned cucumbers and beef, also boxed crackers, cotton covers, a couple bottles cordial, a bottle aspirin, an accurate compass, a big chest containing cocaine, coffee, cheese, caboose also contains a caged cicada, an Austrian chandelier, a couple boxes cigarettes, a castrated cat, a card case, a candelabrum, a cabinet containing African curiosa and awards, a boiler, an ancient blunderbuss, a chained bicycle, a B battery and antenna, a bathtub and a barber's chair, and an anchor, but after a cloudburst boat's cabin ceiling cracks annoyingly. Ceiling collapses. Can't be comfortable anymore. Am closing cabin and after breakfast am continuing crossing coastal area accompanied by a castrated cat. All charts aren't accurate, but according charts bush areas can be avoided by advancing circuitously. After considering all alternatives, I capture a couple crocodiles. Chaining crocs and attaching an abandoned car am carefully advancing. By and by a couple alligators come along, creating a comical convoy. All blacks are a bit aghast, also a bit amused as convoy creeps along.

Am by-passing cities as birds circle above, crying: biu, biu, biu. Afternoon, am asking a couple crouching blacks about a blonde chick, beautiful but a bit battered by age . . . Another cloudburst. Am anxious as an army corporal attests Alva could be anywhere beyond barricades after ants attacked before breakfast and captured a couple Americans . . . After army's counterattack against ants badly blunted, African army consumes bread and butter, also corn and Belgian beer. All complain close-by artillery barrage battered beautiful city, battered beautiful avenues, all because ants continue advance, continue creeping along, carving a continent.

By complete accident come across a courier ant carrying ant code. Crush ant, and alone attempt cracking cipher. Am a bit astonished because apparently code also contains a cou-

146

pon. Calmly concentrate cracking cipher. Code cleverly conceals a choice between cream cheese and chocolate-coated biscuits. Am confounded by clever camouflage. Am also confounded by a Chad colonel's conjecture about Alva's complicity. Colonel claims Alva's charisma assists ants. Bullshit. Colonel, clearly a bloody ass. Although admittedly Alva and both Alex and Allen could command an ant attack. All conceivable but absolutely circumstantial. After another attempt at cracking cream cheese code am convinced ants are creating an African corridor connecting Berbera, Bula Burti and Basongo. Anyhow, am also convinced Alva couldn't be a commander by choice. Ants are captivating but cheerless. Code also contains careful compilations by companies complaining about artillery barrage, complaining about combatants being afraid . . . After I cross a close-by creek, am accepted by barricaded army as a celebrity. Casually bullshit a bit about cracking code and about Alva. Am astonished as all applaud and cheer, and commander cancels a cavalry attack after being advised against cavalry, but consistently brush aside all attempts by colonel at awarding an African Cross. Accept compliments after accepting award, also accompany commander and check brigade at attention. By coincidence am around as corporal comes across an astonishing ant burial chamber containing carved arches and an ant arena. Conclude a breathtaking afternoon as an army cook captured another ant carrying an ant bag containing Alva's description. Could Alva conceivably be behind ants' brutal conquests? Colonel asks. Can't convince anyone, Alva can ball but can't battle. Completely crestfallen after being called a bourgeois bastard. Can't cross creek because boat capsized. Cursing am captured by an ant column. Cornered, can't aim correctly, as ants attack. Actually can't complain . . . ants afterward act correctly. As a captive am chained and carried away. Courage . . .

B

BROKENHEARTED AT BEING AMBUSHED and bound, am also baffled by ants' admirable behavior. Between battles am allowed a banana and a box Burundi biscuits and ant butter. Bittersweet butter awful. Another bright breathtaking autumn afternoon. Am absorbed by ants' brainy behavior . . . and by ants' boldness. Astonishingly, all ant advisers are bilingual. Avoid another blunder by accepting assigned billet, an abandoned army barrack. Barter a brown army belt and an autographed book, and acquire a bench, also bedding and a broken bathtub. All Americans, argues bilingual ant, aren't against an African ant annexation. August auspicious as ants attack. But, ant agrees, Alva almost blameless. Almost?

Am appeasing ants by being awfully appreciative about bench and bedding and also by appearing appropriately apologetic. But as African airforce blasts another aboveground barrack, am betraying anxiety by blabbering and beseeching ants. Bilingual ants are amused. Am afraid ants can't be beaten. Ants beleaguer another African battalion. Apparently, by all accounts, African artillery below average. After another ant assault, barefoot and agitated Africans appear, balancing boxes, and bearing ammunition and bazookas. All are blindfolded by agile ants, and brought back. Am astonished as benevolent aggressors adopt Africans as bearers. Ably barter another belt

148

and acquire a Baedeker and barbiturates. Admittedly, all ants are below average bargainers.

After another bitter biweekly battle Bantus are bankrupt. After battle Bantus begin backing away, begin building boats, begin betraying army by abandoning armed airforce base, as ants advance, annihilating alligators, antelopes and a battling Bantu battalion . . . Am all alone. By betraying an alarm as bombs blasts barracks am assuring ant advisers about being afraid. By all ant accounts Alva and both Alex and Allen are alive. All are assisting ants. Alva by amusing ant army. Alex by burying badly bitten Bushmen and Bantus. Am aware all accusations against Alva are absolutely baseless. Am ashamed at being an author. Accept blame after being accused by ant advisers. Barter another belt and acquire a broom and a brass bowl. Am becoming affluent. Ahhh . . . affluence. But am annoyed and aggravated as bilingual ant adviser asks about Alva's alleged betrothal. By answering, am Alva's betrothed, antagonize ant. Ant asks again about Alva's alleged betrothal. Answering briefly, am accosted by another bigger ant. Am bravely backing away as Alva accompanied by Alex and Allen arrive, bearing a Bunsen burner and a bullfrog. Amazed at Alva's appearance, almost burst, and after almost bursting assist Alex and Allen by busily broiling bullfrog. After an appetizing breakfast, all are amused by a blow-by-blow account about ants' below average bargaining and by ants' bungling bureaucracy. Am appointed adviser by Alva, after advising a breakaway. All are agreed. Barter all belts and acquire a broken bus and burro. Both Alex and Alva against all advice begin attaching bus behind burro, as belted ants arrive, and argue bilingually about allowing a breakaway. But after Alva allows all bilingual ant advisers, ants agree.

149

Bloody brilliant, Alex admits. Bloody brilliant, although all are aggrieved and a bit angry because Alva again allowed all bilingual ants. Alex and Allen briefly argue about Alva's accomplished accommodations . . . as Alva, beautiful Alva, astride a burro assists another burro across a bridge built by an ant battalion. All aboard, bawls Alva. All abo-o-o-ard. Action, action, bloody bastards . . . after bus. Am accompanied by Alex and Allen, both badly bruised by blows. Almost affectionately am bawling: Bye Bye ants . . . as bewildered ants answer: Bye Bye Americans . . .

Baby, admits Alva as bus and burros arrive at airport, authors aren't bad advisers after all. Afterward Alex and Allen are agreeably astonished as Alva boldly announces a betrothal. Ahh Alva. Am anticipating April blossoms.

A

ANOTHER ABBREVIATION another abdomen another abduction another aberration another abhorrent ass another abnormal act another aboriginal another approach another absence another abstraction another abuse another acceptance another accent another accessory another accident another accolade another accomplishment another accord another account another accretion another accusation another ache another action another activity another addiction another address another adieu another adjournment another adjustment another admission another adoration another adult another advance another advantage another adventure another adverb another affair another affectation another affluence another affliction another afternoon another age another agent another aggravation another aggression another aim another alarm another alibi another alias another allegory another allotment another alteration another altar another aberrant another ambiance another ambiguity another ambivalence another ambling ant another amnesty another amount another amusement another anachronism another anagram another analogy another analysis another anatomy another ancestor another ancient answer another anecdote another anemone another anger another angle another anguish another animal another ankle another amulet another annexation another anniversary another annotation another announcement another antelope another antenna an-

151

other anthem another anticipation another anticlimax another antidote another antiquarian another antiquity another antitoxin another anxiety another apartment another ape another aperture another appeal another appendage another appointment another appraisal another Arab another arcade another archaeologist another admirer another army another arrangement another arrival another art another article another assault another assassin another astonishment another asylum another atavism another attack another asymmetry another atmosphere another attempt another attire another attraction another author another autograph another automat another autopsy another autumn another available average another avalanche another avenue another aversion another aviary another avoidance another avocation another avid avowal another awareness another awakening another awesome age another axis another Alva another Alex another Allen another Alfred another Africa another alphabet.